# CASHING OUT

# CASHING OUT

*Win the Wealth Game
by Walking Away*

JULIEN SAUNDERS *and*
KIERSTEN SAUNDERS

PORTFOLIO / PENGUIN

PORTFOLIO / PENGUIN
An imprint of Penguin Random House LLC
penguinrandomhouse.com

Most Portfolio books are available at a discount when purchased in quantity for sales promotions or corporate use. Special editions, which include personalized covers, excerpts, and corporate imprints, can be created when purchased in large quantities. For more information, please call (212) 572-2232 or e-mail specialmarkets@penguinrandomhouse.com. Your local bookstore can also assist with discounted bulk purchases using the Penguin Random House corporate Business-to-Business program. For assistance in locating a participating retailer, e-mail B2B@penguinrandomhouse.com.

ISBN 9780593329559 (hardcover)
ISBN 9780593329566 (ebook)

Printed in the United States of America
1  3  5  7  9  10  8  6  4  2

BOOK DESIGN BY TANYA MAIBORODA

*To our son, Beau—*
*if not for your love, sense of humor, and*
*infectious displays of joy, we wouldn't have found the*
*energy to complete this book. We hope it helps to create a better,*
*more equitable world for you to grow into.*

*Love, Mama and Dad*

# Contents

# Part One

# RETHINK YOUR MONEY

# CHAPTER 1

# Your Wake-Up Call

In 2017, we stumbled upon a statistic that stopped us in our tracks. It was from a report[1] that was making the rounds in the media because of one startling prediction: median Black wealth in the United States was on track to be $0 by the year 2053.

The report painted a grim picture of the shrinking Black American balance sheet and offered historical context for how we got here: the legacy of slavery; disadvantaged school systems; housing discrimination; the racial wage gap; unfair hiring practices, credit scoring, and lending practices; and even domestic terrorism. We were familiar with all these forces individually, but this was the first time we'd ever seen a dollar value and date assigned to the impact of their combined weight.

It was utterly heartbreaking, but it confirmed much of what we suspected to be true: despite outward appearances and a few comforts here and there, most people we knew were flat broke.

Sure, most of them were college graduates who had good jobs with salaries that allowed them to live in beautiful homes and drive luxury cars. But they were completely missing the bigger picture. To earn the big salary, they had to take on huge amounts of debt and embed themselves in workplaces they didn't feel entirely comfortable in. To maintain the appearance of success, they were in significant amounts of revolving credit card debt. And at home, with the little energy they had left after pretending to be someone they weren't, they found themselves exhausted, unable to recognize themselves. Something didn't add up.

At the end of the month, there was little if anything left over and almost nothing going toward saving for the future. After housing, transportation, food, student loans, insurance, and childcare, they'd find themselves questioning whether they could afford to get a side of guacamole with their burrito. They'd wonder where all their money went, whether college was even worth it, and why they didn't feel as good as they thought they would after landing the job of their dreams. It was clear there was a growing disconnect between the pride they felt when they were on the job and the challenges they experienced measuring their overall progress.

In essence, our friends, family, and co-workers were working their butts off to keep their heads above water, proverbial hamsters on a wheel, yet they were going nowhere fast. Even those we knew who had well-paying jobs didn't have much to show for it, because they took on massive student loan debt to get there, sometimes well over $100,000. We'd ask them, "What's the plan?" and their responses were all the same—a collection of flippant, defeated, or wildly optimistic one-liners that were great for pivoting out of uncomfortable conversations but did little to explain how they planned to dig themselves out of a ditch.

"Just gotta keep grinding."

"It is what it is . . . right?"

"If I get into this program, my debt will be forgiven after twenty years of service."

None of these instilled much confidence. Even more concerning was the number of people who believed going back to school and incurring even more debt was the only path to financial freedom. Despite being some of the smartest people we knew, they weren't thinking critically, or at least weren't being honest with themselves. Rather, they were all reading from a script, playing a character in a television drama. You know the one—the friend who projects bravado but underneath it all doesn't like the person they see in the mirror and is deathly afraid of what the future holds.

You may have someone like this in your life. And if you're being completely honest with yourself, that someone may be you. To get ahold of people who have all the intellect but seemingly little courage to act, you need a wake-up call.

## A Quick Introduction

Before we dive in, it's best if we pause for just a moment to introduce ourselves. We're Kiersten and Julien Saunders. After meeting in 2012, we set out on a path to learn as much as we could about money and apply it to our life. In the next five years, we'd go on to achieve complete debt freedom, including paying off the mortgage on our primary home, student loans, credit card debt, car loans, and tax debt. We took it a step further by choosing to self-manage our investment portfolio instead of using a financial adviser, boosted our saving rate, and built a small rental property portfolio in addition to working our corporate jobs. Through frugal living, simple investing, grit, and creativity, we've amassed a net worth that ranks us in the 90th percentile of families in our age-group in the United States.

But our goal has never been to build wealth simply to benefit ourselves. We have a deep love for our community and understand the critical role money plays in helping families build better lives. So through our award-winning blog, podcast, video series, and more, we're focused on inspiring, educating, and empowering as many people as possible to achieve their financial goals.

As you flip through these pages, we'll share everything we've learned with you; you'll learn more about who we are as individuals and as a family. You should also know that for the majority of this book, we'll be speaking in the first person and from a plural point of view. On the few occasions where we do change it up, we'll be sure to let you know so you don't get confused.

## The Wake-Up Call

One night as we were lying in bed preparing to go to sleep, the phone rang. It was Julien's mother, and the strain in her voice indicated something was wrong. She said she was in the emergency room because her blood pressure was high. Even after taking her medication, she hadn't been able to get it down to a normal rate. This wasn't the first time she'd gone to the hospital for this reason, so we were worried.

We attended her next cardiologist visits with her, and while there, we were taken aback by how frank the doctor was. He told her she had two choices: She could lose weight, and as the pounds fell off, he would slowly wean her off the array of medications she was on. Alternatively, she could do nothing. He would keep tweaking her prescriptions until they found an effective treatment plan, and she would sign up for an ongoing battle to find the right blend of pills for the rest of her life.

The doctor was matter-of-fact but charming (in an old Southern Baptist kind of way). He knew when to play dumb, how to gently probe for answers, and when to be the adult in the room. He even shared his story of helping his own mother lose weight so she could live a more fulfilling life in her golden years. But we were most impressed with his ability to set expectations for the coming months. He made it very clear, in no uncertain terms, that she would set the tone for her treatment, not him.

In the middle of all this, Kiersten received similar news. Her father, whom we affectionately call Blue, had been diagnosed with stage 2 cancer. It was a somber and slow conversation where the pauses and silence took up more space than the words. "Well," Blue said in his signature Texas drawl, "it looks like years of living the good life finally caught up with me."

He was careful not to convey too much optimism—he wasn't quite sure that everything *would* turn out okay—but he told us his doctor said his was her "favorite kind of cancer." She reassured him by saying, "You do your part, and I'll do mine."

In two separate situations, two doctors had found a way to help their patients understand the stakes and accept less than ideal solutions. Within weeks, Julien's mom completely changed her diet, tripled the distance she usually walked, and lost several inches around her waistline. Blue started chemotherapy, quit smoking, and gave up alcohol during his treatment. We were relieved, but, perhaps even more so, we were shocked: our parents, in their sixties and seventies, made swift and drastic lifestyle choices for the better. Losing weight and chemotherapy are both notoriously imperfect and uncomfortable solutions. Both required our parents to limit or entirely remove parts of their lifestyle they'd come to enjoy. But with seemingly little persuasion, they found the will to live. And what started as terrifying moments for our family turned into much-needed stories of recovery and resilience.

Once our parents were given a wake-up call (sprinkled with some encouragement and humor), and then given the control of their own destinies, they made life-altering changes. Changes they probably knew they should have made years earlier but for some reason hadn't sunk in. We hope to do exactly that for you. Deliver a bold wake-up call (sprinkled with encouragement and humor) and offer you the reins back to your own financial health.

Now, you may be thinking the stakes for a life-threatening

physical health condition are higher than those for financial health, or that you can treat improving your understanding of money with less urgency. But we believe otherwise. We believe your ability to earn, save, and grow money is central to your quality of life. In fact, the inability to manage your money effectively can have a direct impact on your health and career choices. It can also affect your ability to maintain relationships, support family in need, or take breaks when you need them.

Let's be honest, haven't we all witnessed an increase in GoFundMe campaigns in recent years because families don't have adequate insurance or estate plans? Don't we all know older workers who are staying on the job longer than they originally planned to because they don't have enough retirement savings? Haven't we all seen people work jobs they don't enjoy despite being sick because they need the money? All of these instances are indicators of how fragile life has become for millions of people, yet too many of us are ignoring the problem.

In this book, we'll help you understand and make these connections so that money becomes less of a topic you avoid and more of an everyday habit.

## Math Is Simple. Black Life Isn't.

We know most financial experts have developed their point of view in a world that doesn't look like ours. Of course, you've likely thought, as we have, that hard work, saving, and investing can improve your life. But even if the math adds up, the advice lacks the necessary context that makes it relevant. The math and tactics are simple, but unfortunately Black life isn't.

Getting a good job, climbing the corporate ladder, buying a nice home, growing a successful business, and making financial decisions are incredibly difficult feats for the majority of Black people today. There are different qualitative variables that require us to do emotional calculus while others perform basic arithmetic. This calculus has a tremendous effect on our decision-making process, mental health, risk tolerance, family, and ultimately financial life.

For instance, many of us are all too familiar with having to choose between investing for our own future and giving back to support our parents in their later years. Or having to choose between responding to a child's developmental needs, nurturing a broken marriage, and our own self-care to keep the family afloat. And on top of it all, we earn less than our white peers for doing the same work, we're less likely to be promoted, and we have to deal with a constant slew of microaggressions in predominantly white workplaces. This is why so much of the standard financial and career advice falls on deaf ears. It doesn't acknowledge the other factors that play a huge role in how so many of us earn money.

In this book, we promise not to hide from those touchy subjects; rather, we'll face them head-on and incorporate them into our advice. Just as if you were preparing to climb one of the world's most difficult mountains, we will equip you with guides, alternative routes, resources, and a community of cheerleaders.

This requires us to do more than just tell you what to do. We need to share our experience and the experiences of others whom we've met along the way.

Our journey started on opposite sides of the tracks with one of us being raised in an upper-middle-class household while the other was raised on the edge of poverty. And though we met at the beginning of our professional heights, we were both ill-equipped to navigate managing money, relationships, and our careers at the time. In fact, our very first conversation about money led to our first argument and ultimately a breakup.

But rather than roll over in defeat, we found the will to overcome our differences and vowed to never allow conflicts about money to keep us apart. While learning about managing debt, investing, and entrepreneurship, we explored our respective pasts to understand how we'd come so far yet knew so little about how to properly manage money. And over time, as our lives became more intertwined, we found our rhythm. At our peak, we saved 70 percent of our income in a single year. We owned a cash-flowing rental property that was appreciating handsomely in market value, and we completely renovated our primary home in preparation for it becoming our second rental. We even went so far as to pay off the mortgage on that home on Kiersten's birthday in 2017.

Altogether, between 2013 and 2018, we paid off $200,000 in debt. We were obsessed with debt payoff and wealth building, having completely immersed ourselves in the personal finance community, churning through books, podcasts, documentaries, articles, and blogs. If it had anything to do with money, we were on top of it. Occasionally, we even attended in-person events to gain access to a network of other wealth builders around the country. We were able to support our friends who started business ventures and help people in need. And we did it without sacrificing our own financial stability. We were living the Black American Dream, but we were incredibly naive.

We assumed everybody knew about this stuff. And if they didn't, all we had to do was flip them an email and they'd follow through. But after repeated attempts we realized we needed to take a different approach. Instead of introducing an exhaustive list of new ideas, we needed to meet people where they were. Instead of boring a hole into their heads, we needed to build a path into their hearts. We needed to respect the cultural taboo of talking about money, not trample all over it. So we started sharing stories about our own experiences managing life, paying off debt, transitioning careers, and investing on our blog. Over the years, this blossomed into a podcast and a video series, *Money on the Table*, where we hosted friends over a delicious meal while tackling a financial topic. Almost immediately, our approach resonated with people from all walks of life around the world. We soon began to receive heartfelt messages from readers, listeners, and viewers about how our story and approach helped them to confront their own challenges and improve their financial lives.

In some cases, we were introducing people to entirely new ways of thinking about money. And in others, we were able to help them stop ignoring the harsh and obvious truths they'd grown accustomed to ignoring, like accepting they'd have to work twice as hard for half as much for their entire career. Or that perhaps their chances for getting the promotion they'd hoped for were lower than they thought they were. Through living by example and sharing our story and the stories of others, we were able to help people envision a completely different life from what they'd imagined for themselves.

The result? We've inspired thousands of people to pay off millions of dollars in debt and build a path to financial independence. Most important, we've helped people confront and remove their emotional roadblocks so they can focus on what matters most to them—family.

From vice presidents of companies, to rising stars in entrepreneurship, to leaders of nonprofit organizations, we've seen and heard it all. With each story, we've guided people to a more secure, happy, and balanced way of living. Now we'll share those same lessons with you.

## Win the Game by Cashing Out

When most people hear "cashing out," they envision blackjack, slot machines, or some other form of gambling in a casino. While that isn't our intent, the logic is the same when it comes to money and your career. The goal is to get in, rack up wins, and get out before they kick you out. You don't want to be the person praying over dice at the craps table at three o'clock in the morning any more than you want to be the person who works tirelessly for forty years with nothing to show for it. Today, more than ever before, winning at wealth requires you to know when you're winning and how to position yourself to quit while you're ahead.

In this book, we'll tap into your innermost motivations to build real wealth, provide you with clear guidelines to break free from required work on your own terms, and lead you to an end goal with your dignity and retirement portfolio intact. We'll do this by helping you make sense of investing so you're not so dependent on an expert, adviser, or guru to erode the earnings you've worked so hard for. We'll provide you with a simple framework for managing your career so you can actually envision a life after it. And we'll help you navigate the difficult conversations and tensions that arise whenever life and money intersect. Cashing out is about getting to a point where you don't have to spend so much time obsessed with paying bills, fighting for a promotion, or sacrificing your well-being for money, and instead pour more of your time into doing the things that truly bring you joy.

While much of the advice and counsel offered in this book is relevant to all people, we want to be clear: this book is written from a Black and minority perspective. Why? Because those communities are most in need. And because Black and Brown people are estimated to be the new majority minority in the coming decades, we want to make sure we're equipping them with information and stories that are designed to uplift them. The widening gaps in wealth we see didn't happen overnight, and reversing these trends won't happen overnight either. But together, through a combination of public policy change and radical individual action, we can each begin to construct a brighter, more equitable future. There is no question that there is much work to be done, and while it may seem counterintuitive, the path forward isn't by working harder on the job. It's by cashing out, walking away from uninspiring work, acknowledging the legacy of broken institutional promises, and taking control of your own financial future.

When you're done, you'll have completely eliminated self-defeatist language from your vocabulary and be supercharged to overcome the obstacles in your path. You'll be able to convert all the fire in your belly into more sustainable forms of energy and income. And you'll feel less lonely as you build a plan toward financial freedom because you'll feel connected to people who look like you all around the world.

But none of this will come easily or comfortably. Adopting this new way of thinking and putting these actions into place will require you to make some adjustments and discard foundational beliefs. You'll need to go from believing hard work always pays off to accepting that it doesn't. You'll have to question your obsession with excellence and whether it's even worth the effort. And you'll need to stop viewing conflict in your relationships as a red flag and start seeing it as an opportunity for growth. To help ease the pain, we'll be sure to sprinkle some humor in between the swallowing of those bitter pills. If the 2020 pandemic taught us anything, it's that often we must laugh to keep from crying!

Last, we will speak to *you*. Far too many financial "gurus" deliver a message that communicates "You're financially illiterate, and with a bit of know-how I'll solve all your problems."

You'll find no such message in this book.

Just as our parents knew they should have eaten healthier, exercised more, and given up alcohol and cigarettes long before the doctors told them to, there's a chance you're *already* familiar with some of the advice about achieving financial freedom. You might have heard the stock market is a wealth-building machine and that the only way to win is to have skin in the game. You might have already been introduced to the concept of budgeting and why it's so important to track your expenses. And you may already be wary of climbing corporate ladders. However, it was the doctors' respectful, clear message that empowered our parents to finally change their own physical health. We hope to do the same for your financial health.

So, consider this your wake-up call. The moment you've been waiting for. As you read and apply the lessons in this book, note that they aren't just *our* lessons. They are a collection of financial wisdom, curated from years of hard work, inspiration from others, and research. They're a collection of our personal stories and stories of others designed to challenge and change how you think about money. We've taken all of this and packaged it specifically for our Black community (although anyone can learn from these ideas). But remember, when you're done flipping through it all, the decision to change will always be yours.

## Rules and Richuals

This book is divided into two sections. In Part I, Rethink Your Money, we're addressing the mindset shifts required to take the leap, starting with rejecting the mantra and glitz of Black excellence and embracing the proven sustainability of stealth wealth. In Part II, The Daily Struggle, you'll learn practical strategies for making the most of your money, like creating an investment portfolio, having productive conversations with your partner about money, and finding a supportive community.

The set of beliefs to cash out can be divided into two categories: rules and "richuals."

Rules are just as you understand them to be: strict guidelines, tactics, and approaches that shouldn't change for the foreseeable future. We believe the right answer to almost every financial question should begin with the phrase "it depends," but when it comes to rules, there's little wiggle room. These are the evergreen hills we're willing to die on.

Then there are what we call richuals. Unlike rules, richuals are a bit more flexible. They're general guidelines that can help direct you in complex situations. With richuals you have permission to tweak, apply, or disregard based on your own life. They're especially useful at the intersection between money and relationships, and they're meant to be revisited and evolve over time. They're firm enough to offer some support but not enough to lay a foundation on. If rules are religious texts, richuals are the best friend you lean on to help make a life decision.

At the end of every chapter of this book, we'll include some rules and richuals. These will help you immediately apply what we've discussed.

Will there be some math involved? Of course. Will we put financial analysis at the core of every decision? Absolutely not. Believe it or not, there isn't a number that will make you feel secure, confident, or free; those are all feelings. And if you're anything like the friends and family we've had these conversations with over the years, we're not concerned about your ability to think critically or understand these concepts. We know you're smart. In fact, you're probably too smart. The real challenge is in overcoming shame from past choices, self-doubt, and loneliness and finding the courage to press forward when life punches you in the face. Having more money doesn't solve all of life's problems, but it damn sure makes life easier.

# CHAPTER 2

# Rich and Regular

We knew we had a problem when we were checking our work email during our honeymoon.

We should have been listening to the waves from the Atlantic Ocean as they crashed against the beach to our right. We should have been watching the clouds spill over mountain ranges like vanilla ice cream melting over a warm brownie to our left. Directly in front of us, gorgeous modern homes sprinkled the landscape with their windows aglow from the stunning sunset over Camps Bay. We were nestled in the middle of it all, perched on a balcony in South Africa. And instead of fully basking in the moment, we had our heads buried in our iPhones.

We had made a promise to ourselves that on this trip we would pay attention to each other and leave work behind. But then, just hours before we were to return home, we had both received an email telling us that the head of the organization where we both worked had abruptly resigned. Just like that, we were sucked back in, glued to our screens, missing the beauty that engulfed us. It didn't really matter why he quit. What did matter was our recurring inability to keep a simple commitment to ourselves. Here we were, in one of the most beautiful places on earth, celebrating the beginning of our new life together, and we couldn't unplug. But our relapse should've come as no surprise.

We met at work, so our jobs were always the third wheel in our relationship. Instead of taking our honeymoon immediately after our wedding, we squeezed in five business trips over a six-week stretch. Days before we got engaged, we even found ourselves hunting for muscle relaxers abroad because we'd strained our necks from working hours on the plane. Like you, we took pride in our work ethic, and it's one of the characteristics each of us found attractive in the other. However, over time, we'd allowed our work to define us.

The money was good, but it wasn't our only motivation for working as much as we did. What we really wanted was to be our ancestors' wildest dreams—to embody Black excellence. So if we had to work nights, weekends, and a few hours on vacation every now and then, we would, because our fatigue paled in comparison to the experiences of those who'd paved the road before us. We believed that no matter how uncomfortable or exhausting it became, being the only Black person in the room was a small price to pay if it meant shattering glass ceilings and representing our community to the fullest. But after years of corporate drudgery, answering every ping from work, and dealing with lingering workplace racism, we took a moment to look in the mirror with honesty. Who had we become?

Spending two weeks eight thousand miles away from it all delivered the hard stop that we needed. It was 2015, the United States was reeling from yet another racially fueled political media frenzy, and we were grateful to not be in the middle of it. As our bodies relaxed and work voices faded away, it was as if we were seeing and hearing each other for the very first time. And as we thought about our future together, one thing became abundantly clear: our job titles would not be on our tombstones.

At the end of the day, the standard of Black excellence isn't worth it if it costs you your sanity and your well-being. You deserve to live a life that is designed to put your needs ahead of the endless list of unsolvable problems work forces on you. Imagine a world where your job no longer defines you and you can soak up memorable moments in real time. Imagine the kind of freedom that allows you to thrive without living paycheck to paycheck, at the whims of a corporation prone to racism and layoffs.

Did such a freedom exist for us, the everyday, working Black Americans? The answer was undoubtedly yes, and we knew just where to start. This wasn't about apathy or indifference. It was about bottling up the clarity gained in that moment on that balcony and being able to sip from it whenever we needed to. We'd been keeping an eye on an interesting corner of the personal finance community, and the people there seemed to have figured something out. After we allowed work to invade our honeymoon on another continent, it was time for us to dive in and become more than just casual bystanders.

# Flirting with FIRE

At the time, we knew what retirement was and that we needed to save and invest to get there, but we lacked the kind of specificity that made it feel real. This is because neither of us had many examples of people who'd actually retired successfully. Most of the people we knew who considered themselves retired were either still working part-time jobs or living relatively meager lifestyles. They looked and lived nothing like the silver-haired couples sipping piña coladas on the cover of popular magazines.

This added to our concern because as we tried to imagine what our lives might look like forty years down the road, we had very little to draw inspiration from. It didn't take us long to realize what was really at stake here. If we blindly followed the advice and tactics of our parents' generation, we'd end up just like them—woefully unprepared or unable to retire. This was bigger than not being able to sip fruity cocktails on a beach. It was about advancing our family and community.

We stumbled upon the financial independence and retire early, or FIRE, movement after digging into real estate investing online. The movement can be defined as a group of savvy, unconventional, and mostly self-taught people who were managing their money in a way that allowed them to leave their jobs with little concern about ever running out of money. Many of the people we followed had built massive property portfolios or businesses and were generating more than enough passive income to live comfortably. By also reducing expenses and investing wisely, they were able to amass significant wealth and achieve the freedom we were looking for and in some cases retire early. This FIRE community had somehow found a way to cash out.

Reading their blogs and listening to their podcasts was like watching financial X Games: it was different, shocking, and predominantly white. At first, we chalked it up to something "those" West Coast yuppies did and couldn't envision ourselves or anyone who looked like us choosing this way of life. We thought, if you had a good job, why would you be in such a rush to leave it? And why would you go to such great lengths as living off the grid, not owning a car, or never going out to eat to do it so quickly? We thought we simply didn't have to go to such lengths to achieve similar goals. But as we dug deeper, our perspective changed.

## WHAT DOES FIRE MEAN?

The FIRE acronym can be broken into two parts: financial independence (FI) and retire early (RE). The traditional version of FI requires that you spend significantly less than you make and invest the difference until you build an investment portfolio that generates enough income to live on for the foreseeable future. That's it. Those who pursue this way of life operate with a fundamentally different problem-solving tool kit. The spirit of FIRE is that you can always have more with less. Way, way less.

Like veganism, we didn't simply dismiss the merits of the lifestyle because it seemed unfamiliar, unnecessary, or extreme.

While these people seemed extreme, many of them were rich enough that they could afford the freedom we wanted. And, more interestingly perhaps, they were regular: they weren't celebrities, athletes, or trust fund kids. They painted a picture of wealth that seemed achievable, albeit at a cost.

After our experience in South Africa, we had to give ourselves a gut check. Did we really think we could keep up this pace? Did we believe we had another thirty years in the tank? Would the company we worked for even exist that long? If it didn't, where else would we go? Would we ever need to leave home for a job opportunity? We had to confront our beliefs, commitments, and desires about building wealth while working in corporate America. There was little evidence to suggest we, as Black professionals, would have long careers, be paid fairly, and be granted the right to compete for the best-paying jobs. And if we did, we weren't confident our experience in those environments wouldn't have long-lasting effects on our physical and mental health.

We had to get really honest with ourselves: the direction we were headed in would never help us get *out* of a cycle of working for others and giving up our financial futures to a career. To make the kind of progress we were truly envisioning, we had to be willing to think and act differently. Cashing out wasn't about giving up. It was about letting go.

Our self-reflection ultimately led us to five compelling reasons to cash out.

## 1 | *More Time to Do What You Love*

If we asked you to make a list of what was most important in your life, we're willing to bet family and community would be near the top of the list. We're no different, and like you we struggled to make the connection between how we managed our time amid a growing list of competing priorities. Contrary to the messaging that shaped our early understanding of money, building wealth wasn't this inherently selfish act. Rather, it was a pathway to our achieving a degree of freedom that had long felt out of reach. Knowing this, we've designed our life in a way that is centered on our financial priorities in the earlier parts of our careers. This prevents us from perpetually ignoring the roles family, community, purpose, faith, and sustainability play in our lives as we get older.

When we were traditionally employed, our jobs required us to travel up to 40 percent of the year, and we had both taken on the classic "road warrior" persona, jockeying for airline status and comparing airport club lounges as pillow talk. We were never as annoying as the people who immediately stood up and crowded the aisles once the plane landed, but if we were at a dinner party and you saw our heads bowed, chances are we were staring at our screens instead of saying grace.

Our smartphones created a sense of faux connectedness to the not-so-real world. Almost 80 percent of our waking hours were spent either at work or thinking about work, and almost everything else went on the calendar. And we mean just about everything *wink.* If spontaneity was a key ingredient for a romantic marriage, needless to say, we were a few fries short of a Happy Meal.

On occasion we drove to work together but rarely enjoyed the commute. On rides home we talked about work, during dinner we talked about work, and on Saturday mornings we savored coffee together as we reflected on not being at work. To our credit, we did book our vacations far in advance, but that was mostly because it was less expensive and because if we didn't, we were prone to join the 55 percent of Americans who don't use all their vacation time.[1]

If it wasn't on the calendar, it simply didn't get done. We talked about time as if optimizing it were the only option, and as if it were precious sand slipping from our fingers. Meanwhile, our financially independent friends who weren't trading time for money discussed how they spent their days as an expression of their values. It was almost poetic. They spent tons of time with their partners and especially enjoyed the little things like a slow hot breakfast, late morning walks, or midweek lunch dates on the other side of town. Beyond their interpersonal lives, cashing out enabled them to dig deep into their interests and in several cases become experts in their fields of study. Watching their days unfold eventually expanded the way we thought about wealth building. In a weird way, it became a means to protect our marriage by insulating it from the leading cause of divorce (money) and giving us ample opportunities to nurture our love without distraction.

## 2 | *Safety from Constant Corporate Change*

The C-suite officer who'd left work had become the latest in a cycle of highs and lows filled with bloated expectations, frequent reorganizations, and thin promises of a new, sharper vision. We watched the old guard get thrown out like rusted tools, and every time leaders would passionately express how confident they were that *this* time we were "more aligned than ever."

This ever-revolving seat of leaders wasn't unique to our company or industry. In fact, it was part of a larger trend of leadership exits across all sectors. At the end of 2017, the average CEO tenure was only seven years, and even that number was skewed by a few notable examples who had been in roles for more than twenty years. By 2019, CEO turnover reached a record high, and not only were they leaving more frequently, but they were also staying in their roles for shorter periods of time.[2]

With each new leader came a new vision, which stifled our abilities to do our jobs. And if we dared to express frustration about the constant change, it was consistently reframed as our inability to adapt. We'd be encouraged to build the plane while we were flying it, or iron our shirts while we were still wearing them. Shareholders wanted to see growth, and we were tasked with getting it done despite shrinking budgets, hiring freezes, and a lack of cross-functional alignment.

As much as corporate leaders talk about "sticking together," there is no camaraderie when people's livelihoods are at stake. Cashing out flips the script on this kind of workplace turbulence and puts you back in charge of your choices. When organizational changes inevitably happen, you can choose to walk away instead of sitting at the table fighting for scraps.

### 3 | *Increased Likelihood of Success—*
### *on Your Own Terms*

Though exhausting, we'd become skilled at climbing the corporate ladder over the years. But once we actually looked up and saw the faces at the top, it was clear that almost nobody looked like us. Like many of our colleagues, we'd spent a lot of time working on our professional development, networking, and boosting the image of the company to outsiders. We participated in and in some cases built employee resource groups to influence the company strategy and increase diversity in leadership. We did this in addition to our primary responsibilities for no increase or adjustment in pay, only to consistently see more white outsiders come in and take the helm.

In theory, frequent leadership turnover implies there is room to hire more diverse candidates. But after witnessing countless, talented Black colleagues routinely passed up for promotions, we'd begun to believe meritocracy was as mythical as Santa Claus. We were perpetually over-appreciated and underpaid. Instead of receiving pay or positions, we were given awards and applause. And as we dug into the data, the evidence was more damning: in 2019, only 3.2 percent of senior leadership positions and 0.8 percent of Fortune 500 CEO spots were held by Black professionals.[3] This meant our chances were only slightly better than a high school basketball player making it to the NBA and that the few people who'd done it were outliers.

We spent years casually joking about white mediocrity, but these odds led us to heartbreaking new conclusions about Black excellence.

The fact is, despite your best efforts to assimilate, the likelihood a business leader would ever look you in the eye and say "you remind me a lot of myself when I was your age" are slim to none. Even in the face of all the diversity and inclusion efforts of the last decade, Black people are still more likely to be put in a commercial than in a corner office. And there are simply too many structural and systemic barriers to believe working hard at a job will net anything beyond unpaid overtime. It's clear that adopting the principles of FIRE has the potential to create more Black millionaires than corporate America ever could.

## 4 | *Create the Family You Want*

We were child-free back in 2015, but even at that point in our careers we were starting to find the constant use of familial language disingenuous. It's one thing for peers to affectionately refer to each other as "work fam," a title given to people based on genuine friendships and earned through mutual trust. It's another thing to hear leaders co-opt "family" to create a false sense of security to unite us after massive layoffs.

So, when we thought about the busyness of our lives, we weren't sure how kids would fit in the picture. Time and time again we'd listen to senior executives say their family was the most important thing to them in talks about how they achieve the elusive work-life balance, only to list "spending more time with family" as the reason for their departures. As Kiersten's dad likes to say, "That dog don't hunt."

Corporate America gives a lot of lip service about how important family is while not providing much support. In 2020, a marketing agency collected data from thirty trusted sources to create the "Raising a Family Index" (RAFI).[4] They used the RAFI to determine the most and least family-friendly countries and ranked thirty-five wealthy nations according to safety, happiness, cost, health, and time. The United States ranked second to last overall and scored the worst in time, which was calculated by looking at the number of hours worked and paid time off for vacation days, parental leave, and sick days.

The survey confirmed what we already felt to be true— that Americans don't have enough time to raise a family. The data shows that only 38 percent of U.S. organizations offer paid leave, and of the parents who receive it, the average length at full pay is only four weeks. Once parents head back into the office, those with an average household income spend nearly one-third of it on childcare costs alone.[5]

Continuing to work as hard as you do with no end in sight to provide for a family you don't get to see is ass backwards. By cashing out, you can create the space, money, and time you need to truly prioritize the people you love.

# 5 | *Freedom from Burnout*

Ignoring uncomfortable truths is as American as apple pie. We'd benefited from employee turnover over the years but soon realized that by design we were on the conveyor belt to the trash bin ourselves. We'd seen a handful of other Black superstars rise and fade away, unable to find a reasonable path upward. Those who somehow did find a way wore the evidence of their sacrifice on their sleeves and privately warned us about the pitfalls of being a pioneer. The true cost of being the first was being the only.

When we huddled at the watercooler with work colleagues or at a social outing with friends, we all seemed to have similar frustrating stories about work and how much of an elaborate ruse it all was. Instead of sharing stories about breaking through barriers, we exchanged busy buzzwords and hacks to maintain the illusion of productivity. And as far as we could tell, there wasn't a single example of someone who'd actually found the ever-elusive work-life balance. Either they'd accepted the limits of their growth and given their all to their families, or they poured their entire selves into work with reckless abandon. How much more quantitative and qualitative evidence did we need? We were surrounded by data that suggested modern management practices and workplaces were directly responsible for a laundry list of stress-induced ailments. We saw firsthand many of our former colleagues struggle with weight gain, neck and back issues, carpal tunnel, and burnout. To make matters worse, as Black employees, we were also likely to earn less for the same work and be promoted less frequently.

Before Big Tobacco put warnings on cigarettes, the list of evidence was just as long. Public opinion didn't start to shift until President Eisenhower, famous for smoking four packs of cigarettes a day, collapsed on vacation. His heart attack caused the stock market to plummet $14 billion in a single day.[6]

What has to happen before we connect the dots between public health and work? Do we need a big scary name for it? In Japan they call it *karoshi*—death caused by overwork or exhaustion. According to a *Business Insider* article, "In the US, 16.4% of people work an average of 49 hours or longer each week. In Japan, more than 20% do."[7]

From climate change and nutritional standards, to the health benefits of cannabis and extreme wealth inequality, to the struggle for civil rights and the current push for economic empowerment, America has proven how gifted it is at ignoring the truth until there is little choice left. What was true for Big Tobacco rings true for almost every other progressive movement of our times: people often need deeply compelling visuals to be moved to action. Whatever your self-care routine is, it's our hope this book helps to make it a central part of your life, not just a pesky line item in your budget.

The data and trends are clear. Doubling down on your ambitious career is *not* the ticket to freedom you are searching for. You need to take control of your full income-earning potential and not assume you will earn an above-average salary for a forty-year stretch. You need to earn income and build wealth while minimizing damage to your health and family structure. Following the standard approach is unreliable, so you need to get creative and take matters into your own hands. The time and energy you are currently pouring into getting promoted needs to be redirected to activities that put your needs first.

## What Is Financial Freedom?

The term "financial freedom" is often thrown around to describe the lifestyles of the rich and famous. Have you ever googled the term "rich"? When we did, we weren't surprised by what we saw: tech entrepreneurs, real estate moguls, and media giants all dressed in well-tailored suits and wearing glitzy jewelry. Of course, there were *also* tons of Leonardo DiCaprio memes from *The Wolf of Wall Street* as he toasted and made it rain off a yacht. The mass media has so expertly crafted extreme images for rich people that any deviation from that visual aesthetic calls into question whether someone is rich at all.

This is especially true for Black people. For us, we're fed images of Black athletes and entertainers in their fancy homes, with their impressive car collections and luxury watches. Unfortunately, the image of wealth we're accustomed to does little to inspire regular people, because it's so detached from reality it's not worth trying to replicate. Most people will willingly pontificate for hours about the subtle difference between rich and wealthy, propping their entire argument on something they've heard from an interview or a Chris Rock comedy routine. All the while, they're completely ignoring the vast land between being where they are (working class) and being rich. They completely skip over that life without realizing it's pretty sweet too.

We have nothing against enjoying expensive things, but the questions we asked ourselves were, Where are all the regular rich people? Where are the people who were rich by all standards but didn't align with the image the media presented to us? Where are the people enjoying the perks of freedom, but not flaunting it? In line with one of our favorite personal finance books, where are the *Black* millionaires next door?

What we've found over the years is that most of us want the freedom that riches bring, but we don't want to change our identity. We want to be seen for our inner light, not our outer bling. We don't want to have to discard our self-identity or abandon our social circles. We don't want to monitor stock tickers all day, spend our evenings finding properties or weekends hustling. We want simplicity, proven results, and confidence that what we are doing is *working*. And that's the essence of what it means to be rich and regular.

In reality, a financially free life for most people looks completely different from the online images. There aren't yachts, designer bags, and a collection of sports cars in every color outside. Financial freedom looks more like taking your sweet time every morning to enjoy a cup of coffee, taking a leisurely afternoon jog after lunch, or scheduling a vacation at a time of year that's most convenient for you, not just when it's most affordable. And honestly, from where we sit now, we can tell you: it's pretty boring. Most of the rich people we know live remarkably predictable lives. They drive regular cars, read often, exercise, travel for long periods, and spend loads of energy diving deep into issues that matter to them. But this type of freedom can't be achieved without letting go of the largest obstacle that consumes the majority of our time—work.

For us, cashing out looked like quitting a well-paying job because the work environment was toxic. It eventually allowed us to swoop into our parents' lives when they were sick without asking anyone for days off or using vacation time. It meant that even before we quit our traditional jobs, we were good at what we did because we were focused on actually doing the job well, instead of mastering the political games that might get us promoted. Most important, cashing out made us more comfortable speaking up about the social issues that mattered to us without fear that doing so might impact our career trajectory or income potential. It afforded us the time we needed to nurture our relationship as a married couple and parents. Today, our version of being rich isn't just about having nice things; it's about living a life aligned with our values devoid of a constant goose chase after money. And that's precisely what we want for you.

We've seen firsthand what the pursuit and achievement of financial independence can do to a family. We've seen the compounding effect of this newfound freedom on extended families, local communities, organizations, and small businesses. We firmly believe that a world with more financially independent people will lead to broader improvements in society because once money isn't the primary focus in your life, other priorities will take its place.

# Three Principles of Cashing Out

*I love America more than any other country in the world, and, exactly for this reason, I insist on the right to criticize her perpetually.*

—JAMES BALDWIN

America has always been, if nothing else, a nation of believers. American citizens are taught to have faith in this country as early as grade school when we are instructed to put our hands over our hearts and pledge allegiance to the flag. It continues into adulthood as we stand for the national anthem during sporting events and line up to vote for our nation's leaders. But for Black people, the acceptance of this sense of duty is complicated because our faith in this country and our faith in a higher power are intertwined. Our churches and mosques have been sacred spaces for both civic activity and racial progress, so it should come as no surprise we often conflate the two.

According to the Pew Research Center report *Faith Among Black Americans*, more than three-quarters of Black Americans say that Black churches have helped promote racial equity.[8] It's no wonder that many of our most revered civic leaders have also been religious leaders. Our faith isn't just the primary tool for our spiritual practices; it's what we bravely step out on whenever we're confronted with problems that are bigger than us.

Now, if you're a Christian, you're probably familiar with the concept of the Father, Son, and Holy Ghost. It's a foundational belief that's intended to teach Christians how complex God is.

It remains one of the most difficult parts of the religion to understand logically, nevertheless we accept it spiritually and emotionally. Well, if you're Black and want to cash out, there is a different trinity you must grow comfortable with: stealth wealth, the Black tax, and purpose and community.

Accepting these three principles is an exercise in untangling your civic faith from your religious faith. You can believe wholeheartedly in your God without believing wholeheartedly in your country. Similarly, you must position yourself to benefit from America's systems without wholly endorsing its flaws. Because developing your financial plan with these principles at the heart of your decision-making requires you to believe that you deserve better than the status quo.

## 1 | *Stealth Wealth*

We were attending CampFI when we heard a term we'd never heard before: "stealth wealth." At that point, it had been four years since our wake-up call in South Africa. We'd been interested in financial freedom for several years and were gaining traction on our financial independence journey.

CampFI is exactly what it sounds like—a camp for people interested in the financial independence lifestyle. Of the thirty attendees, we were two of the five people of color. We were admittedly cautious because the campsite required us to drive through the backwoods of south Georgia and northern Florida: known hotbeds of racism. Thankfully, we arrived safely without any hiccups and were immediately welcomed by the camp's attendees. After the first day of talks and getting to know our fellow attendees, we all hung out on the porch together. Our conversations centered on money and swapping financial hacks. It felt good to be around people who'd overcome the social taboo of talking about money and shared similar philosophies.

While chatting, one of the campers used the term "stealth wealth." He spoke about financial security, helping family members whenever he wanted, and enjoying his job but not feeling pressured to keep it.

To him, having stealth wealth implied you were doing well by all standards but you displayed little, if any, outward appearances of excessive wealth. His wealth was real, measurable, and growing without his lifting a finger, but it was also hardly noticeable to the naked eye. It was certainly unlike the mass-produced images of wealth portrayed in the media. After all, he drove a Subaru hatchback and wore simple athleisure and a dingy pair of New Balance sneakers. His wealth wasn't a game of show-and-tell, and when it was shown, it was visible through the freedoms and conveniences he enjoyed, not the things he consumed. We were in love!

To understand why stealth wealth is so important, you first need to fundamentally believe your money can work harder than you can. Despite the unfortunate stereotypes that have plagued our community for years, we are incredibly hard-working and resilient people. In fact, the legacy of the United States is built on the value of our ancestors' labor. But our community's attachment to that narrative has caused us to overvalue our work ethic. We've been so conditioned to work hard that we don't recognize there are several other ways to earn income that don't require never-ending, backbreaking work.

Also, high earners are prone to "lifestyle inflation." With every milestone or boost in income comes a corresponding upgrade. Graduated from college? Buy yourself a nicer car to acknowledge your achievement. Got married? Buy a bigger house . . . something you can "grow into." Interviewing for a new job? Update your wardrobe because you must look the part to get the part.

While they've accomplished a lot, high earners often have little to show for it, because each additional dollar goes toward paying off what they had purchased to celebrate the milestone—sometimes before they'd even crossed the finish line.

Understanding stealth wealth doesn't mean you never buy yourself anything nice; it simply means you think differently about each new dollar. It means that even when you do get a significant boost in income, you don't spend every penny. Rather, you invest it, with the goal of multiplying it. You find greater joy in watching your money grow over time than you do in buying things you'll eventually outgrow or lose interest in. It's about doing well but keeping it on the low, stealth-like.

## 2 | *The Black Tax*

Many of you who've stumbled upon our blog or picked up this book have likely already acknowledged this truth but haven't fully accepted its impact: despite valiant efforts, racism still plagues every aspect of our lives, and we can't afford to let blind optimism get in the way of progress. Money is no exception.

This means we can't take blanket rules of thumb at face value; rather, we must add a Black tax. Is buying a home a fundamental pillar to building wealth? Yes, but the likelihood of a property substantially appreciating in value in Black neighborhoods is significantly less than in white neighborhoods. Is gaining a higher education key to getting a good job? Sure, but getting your foot in the door as a Black person has far more twists, pitfalls, and potholes than white peers will experience. Is starting a business a pathway to building wealth? Absolutely, but if your business requires funding or a loan from a bank, you are less likely to be approved or to receive competitive terms if you're Black.

We've had to accept these truths; otherwise, we'd be leading people down a path they weren't prepared for. Our commitment to our community requires us to be honest, and you must also be honest with yourself. This isn't about giving up or giving in; it's about incorporating history and data into decision-making. We can't continue to over-rely on prayer, anger, or might as levers to create change. In today's day and age, social change requires funding, so the richer Black people are, the more sustainable our broader efforts become.

## 3 | *Purpose and Community*

When most people think about Dr. Martin Luther King Jr., they think about his famous "I Have a Dream" speech. But Dr. King and his message were so much more than those four words and the handful of other phrases that have underscored his legacy.

In 1962, he wrote a speech titled "The Case Against 'Tokenism'" in which he argued that token integration would not satisfy African Americans because "a new sense of somebodiness and self-respect" had permeated the Black community and driven Blacks to "achieve freedom and human dignity" at all costs. He began the speech by sharing his experience being jailed after a peaceful protest in Albany, Georgia. Dr. King refused to pay the $178 fine and began to settle into serving his forty-five-day sentence when he was bailed out by anonymous donors. In 2020 dollars, that fine would've been approximately $700.

Here's our questions: Who were the donors? Were they celebrities, small-business owners, church leaders, or landowners? Regardless of whether they were Black, white, Asian, or Hispanic, they chose to part ways with their money to advance a cause. To us, that simple and generous act is motivation enough to pursue a financially independent lifestyle.

Many people feel silenced by their jobs and are afraid to speak out about the causes they believe in because they fear doing so could jeopardize their employment. But when you become financially independent, you can more closely align how you spend your time and money with your values. You don't have to worry about anyone taking away your livelihood because you stood up for what you believe in. Even if your efforts are local, money can solve problems. The act of building wealth isn't just a way for you to enjoy nice things; it allows you to leave the world in a better condition.

CASHING OUT ISN'T ABOUT GLAMOUR. It's about intentional spending and leveraging the power of investing to do good. It's about accepting that money impacts every aspect of our life, and whether we like it or not, so does our racial identity. It's about empowering you to keep your word with yourself and, in troubling times, to speak without fear of risking your financial livelihood. It's an individual solution to an institutional problem: a simple financial plan that acknowledges your full self and puts you in control of your life.

This book is written and designed to give you the sense of alignment you're searching for. Making bold financial decisions often creates conflict in our lives because there are often competing objectives. The decision to pay off debt can have a negative impact on your role as a parent or your ability to nurture a romantic relationship. Choosing to leave a job can have a direct impact on your desire to support a parent, church, or cause you believe deeply in. Finding that perfect balance has the tendency to feel impossible, which is why it's so important to be grounded in a set of core values to guide your thinking along the way.

Take a moment and reflect on the decisions, actions, and sacrifices that got you where you are today. Now be honest with yourself. Aren't you tired? Aren't you exhausted from the constant grind, the endless attempts to create some semblance of work-life balance without completely discarding your sense of ambition? You can design a life that enables you to rest without fear that jumping off the hamster wheel will lead to catastrophe. If you're not tired, well, we have news for you: you will be someday. Prepare yourself for the inevitable day your body and mind begin to slow down. We want to ensure that even the laziest version of yourself can live comfortably, confidently, and worry-free about having enough.

## rule

- **Empowerment is an inside job.** Deciding to pursue financial independence is no different from deciding to switch careers, train for a marathon, or build a life with a partner. It begins with you recognizing that better is possible and that you have full authority to push your life into a different direction.

## richual

- **Ignore the pressure to always be positive.** In life, you can't effectively solve problems you aren't honest about. For example, it's okay to look at your career trajectory or business endeavor and decide "this won't end well" after several failed attempts. But to reach this determination, you must be willing to confront uncomfortable truths about yourself, a manager, the company, or an industry. Remember, both negativity and positivity can be toxic.

# CHAPTER 3

# The Purpose(s) of Income

W e've all been there. You grind through a period of time where you're deprived of the things you desire or need. You hang in there for as long as it takes, convincing yourself it will all be worth the wait until you're finally able to have the thing you've been dreaming of. And then . . . the moment comes. You finally make the purchase, and as you begin to experience it for the first time, your brain is flooded with feelings of relief, gratitude, joy, and happiness all at once. Some people liken this sensation to drugs, sex, or falling in love. Others find it therapeutic or compare it to a spiritual experience. Whatever you call it, this cocktail of emotions is incredibly rewarding and feels damn good.

But there's a catch. Now that you've had a sampling of this once forbidden elixir, it's impossible to ignore the memory. You want more and you want more now. And to make matters worse, savvy marketers with droves of data at their fingertips can easily craft messages that bring you right back to the very moment that craving was fulfilled. In a sense, you become addicted to spending money to feel good and find yourself in a constant chase of that high.

This is your brain on consumerism, and it has wreaked havoc on the purses, wallets, and credit scores of millions of people around the country. It's a key contributor to why the average personal saving rate is so low in the United States, why revolving credit card balances are so high, and why so many people aren't able to cover the cost of emergencies without going into more debt.

We wish we could offer you a mantra, patch, or trial period in a treatment center to curb your desires, but unfortunately those don't exist. And sure, you could live off the grid, avoid technology altogether, and use cash to minimize the flood of marketing messages pointed in your direction, but we're not confident that would solve the problem either. Over the years, we've learned that your greatest defense to avoid being trapped in a cycle of consumerism is to have a solid foundation of values, a community you can lean on for support, and rock-solid beliefs that guide your thinking about money. And most important, you need to have a clear purpose for your income—an assignment it's ordered to fulfill.

While giving a talk to students, staff, and faculty at Auburn University, we asked the question, "What is the purpose of income?" Immediately, the room fell silent as if someone farted in church. Some probably thought it was a trick question, while others were too intimidated to attempt an answer. But many had simply never thought about it.

Most people outside that room haven't given much thought to that question either. We have been actively trained to pursue income and define what a "good income" is, but we've never given much thought to its *purpose*.

Much like finding a life's purpose, having a purpose for your income sets the tone for everything you do. Because one thing is clear. If you don't give your income a purpose, someone else will. And their purpose for your income may not be in your best interest.

## Three Types of Financial Personalities

To understand money's true purpose, we must first break down the different ways we view its role in our lives and how it informs our approach, for better or for worse. In the past few years, we've had thousands of conversations about money with people all around the world. In the process, we've identified three clear patterns of financial beliefs and habits—or personalities—based on the way people ask questions, view problems, and practice avoidance. We've given them names: the Financially Insecure, the Fast Spenders, and the Middle.

Grouping people in this way isn't about characterizing them by virtue, income level, or class. It's about acknowledging the commonalities in their approach to managing money.

### 1 | *The Financially Insecure*

For the Financially Insecure, life is unbelievably hard, and they see the world through a repeated presence of struggle. This outlook has made them deeply skeptical and sets the tone for almost every interaction they have. More often than not, they live paycheck to paycheck and perpetually have "more month at the end of their money." They've grown accustomed to this way of life, and their goal is simple: to have enough. It's important to note that financial insecurity isn't always a result of low income, but obviously there is a greater tendency for people with low income to be Financially Insecure.

In 2019, we were cast members of the documentary *Playing with FIRE* and sat on a panel after the film's premiere. During the question-and-answer session, one woman stood up and asked us, "How do you reach financial independence when you have hereditary debt?"

We were unclear on what she meant by this because we'd never heard the term before, but quickly realized she was referring to the generational cycle of poverty. She told us that she came from a tough environment, was still surrounded by it, and was trying to envision financial independence as a way out for everybody in her circle, not just her. She was having a hard time conceptualizing how this foreign concept could work, but there wasn't a data point or suggestion we could offer that she wouldn't dismiss. In her mind, no matter what we said or did, struggle would be an ever-present cloud over her head.

The reality is, for many of the Financially Insecure, there are powers and circumstances at play that make their lives more difficult than most could ever imagine. Medical or legal debt, undereducation, rising costs, mental health struggles, financial responsibility for a large family, childcare for their own children and/or a relative, and living in an economically depressed area are just a few of the barriers many financially insecure people face. Because of this, they adopt a worldview based on the grim realities of life they experience every single day. Over time, some even tend to define themselves by their struggle and take tremendous pride in their survival skills. Having lived through it and having several friends and family members who still are, we completely empathize with those in this predicament.

Look, we believe in the principles we're outlining in this book. But we won't join the chorus of gurus chanting that all you need to do is follow your passions and pick yourself up by your bootstraps. While there are certainly examples of remarkable success to point to, the unfortunate reality is that for some people financial independence will always be a dream out of reach. For some, their circumstances are so dire it requires a comprehensive plan, a social safety net, a complete uprooting of one's life, and good old-fashioned luck. But it also requires a willingness to accept, focus on, and work toward life's possibilities.

When you're drowning in negativity, holding on to a life raft will almost certainly ensure your survival in the short run. But making it ashore or aboard a vessel requires a completely different set of skills and actions, the first of which is believing that a better life is possible.

## 2 | *The Fast Spenders*

Fast Spenders are a truly unique group and have life experiences most people can only dream of. They have a completely different relationship with money, and as the name suggests, it's all about speed. Money both comes in and goes out at such a fast pace there's no time to build an emotional attachment to it and little incentive to try tracking it.

Most people get excited about having money, but what Fast Spenders experience is completely different. They get an all-encompassing, full-spirited rush from spending money, and the desire to do it over and over sets the tone for their lives. Many Fast Spenders are also high earners and tend to work as specialists, consultants, lawyers, high-end real estate developers, or fringe entrepreneurs, which affords them the luxury of spending large amounts of cash freely and quickly. YOLO (you only live once) is their mantra, and in their world money flows wild and free as the wind.

One of our dearest friends is a Fast Spender. He's wildly intelligent, is gainfully employed in the pharmaceuticals industry, and lives in one of the highest cost-of-living areas in the country. He has the stunning ability to earn and burn income, and is unable to meaningfully save for his future. For him, going out for expensive drinks with friends, luxury vacations, exclusive access, and fancy restaurants are all far more intriguing than funding a retirement account. Plus, he believes that if he *wanted* to, he could start saving money tomorrow.

The problem is, tomorrow never comes.

Instead of saving, he finds himself in search of a better job and a bigger paycheck every few years. After a decade of earning obscene amounts of money, he still has massive student loan debt, and as he enters his peak earning years, he has only a few thousand dollars saved for retirement. When we ask him what the plan is, he jokingly admits, "One day, I'm gonna get my shit together . . . Just don't ask me when!"

### 3 | *The Middle*

Most people we meet are what we call the Middle. As you might have guessed, the name is inspired by the socioeconomic category the middle class, which is what most Americans self-identify as. We find this group to be the most interesting because their belief systems and habits are more malleable than those of the other two groups. They know better is possible; they just aren't sure how to get there. They know money and time are precious but admit to taking both for granted every now and then. Because of this, on any given day, they can experience a full range of emotions about money. One minute, they're feeling stuck and frustrated; the next minute, they're comfortable and grateful.

Life for the Middle isn't as painful as that for the Financially Insecure nor as sexy as the life of Fast Spenders. Yet it is highly motivated by experiences in and observations of the other two groups. Put another way, what the Middle sees from the Fast Spenders and the Financially Insecure shapes their thinking and spending decisions.

For instance, the Middle views a 10 percent saving rate as good, even if it's not enough, because they remember the days they weren't able to save nearly as much. The Middle also believes having a big home with a yard and fancy car is a marker of success because that's the image of wealth they've seen in the media. It doesn't matter if the house is ridiculously expensive to maintain or impossible to sell. Some people in the Middle remember what it felt like to be Financially Insecure, so the source of their underlying motivation is to never go back. While life in the Middle may not be awe-inspiring, there is great comfort in knowing they've made enough progress to break free from the grips of insecurity. And as they earn more money, the Middle often find themselves motivated by the hope that one day they can be as carefree as they believe Fast Spenders are. In fact, the taste levels of the Fast Spenders often set the tone for the Middle's desires and temptations.

One defining characteristic of the Middle is they lack perspective on what money can do for them. People in the Middle often have enough income and are even saving for retirement, but they have no idea what they're saving for, how close to or how far they are from achieving that goal, or why they're even doing it. They're often just going through the motions with no clear plan for their life and as a result, no purpose for their income. And when your income lacks purpose, you're vulnerable—vulnerable to being sucked into the system of consumerism and the endless work culture of jobs.

The vast majority of people in the Middle have adopted an approach to thinking about money that gets them only halfway to their anticipated destination. They're doing well, but they can't help but feel haunted by the sense they could or should be doing better. And the way they've defined doing better sets the tone for how they think about their current and future income. In short, they subscribe to the belief that the sole purpose of their income is to afford them the ability to buy better things and experiences. While certain levels of income do give you that ability, that's not its only purpose.

The Financially Insecure and the Fast Spenders, are both worthy of attention and analysis, but are not the focus of this book. Instead, we'll focus our attention on the Middle—the group that includes the most people.

## BUT FIRST, A NOTE ON INCOME AND BLACK BUYING POWER

We've led many impassioned conversations about wealth and how essential it is to driving social change, particularly in the Black community. And whenever we do, we can rest assured someone will mention Black buying power.

"Black buying power" is a frequently used and well-intended talking point meant to emphasize the role money plays in improving Black communities. The statistic is often used as a show of might— a hammer of sorts—with the potential to shatter oppressive institutions. Pundits will argue that we need to vote with our dollars and use Black buying power to demand respect, access, and justice. These moments afford Black people the rare opportunity to promote big-dollar values and claim them as our own. Black buying power becomes a badge of honor, a symbol of possibility, though unfortunately it is a number that is regularly taken out of context and highlights the pervasive misunderstanding of income's purpose.

When most people visualize this number, they imagine taking the collective earned income of every Black person in America to a hypothetical mall where they can buy anything and solve any problem in any community. *What **can't** you afford when you have $1.3 trillion?*[1] they think. *How can the Black community have so much power yet still have so many problems?*

Don't worry, we're not about to dive into mind-numbing economic and social policies. The point is, in our everyday lives the buying power of any demographic isn't relevant. If anything, buying power is a giant "Hot Now" Krispy Kreme donut sign enticing hungry corporations and advertisers to your wallet. The "power" in question has little to do with economic weight or impact, and it certainly doesn't translate to actual wealth, autonomy, or freedom. It literally means the ability of a group of people to spend money (or credit) on specific goods or services. Corporations and marketers use it as a gauge to determine how much they should spend on marketing to attract buyers.

In chapter 1, we noted the report predicting that the median wealth of Black families in the United States will be $0 by 2053 if the racial wealth gap is left unaddressed.[2] And we know that report was produced in 2017, without any insight into how the pandemic might have accelerated the decline of wealth in Black America.

So, how can the African American community simultaneously possess more than a trillion dollars (and growing) in spending power while also have a rapidly declining net worth, on its way to $0? The coexistence of these two contrasting figures illustrates two key points.

First, we must look at these numbers relative to something else. While $1.3 trillion is a large amount of money, that figure by itself is meaningless if it's not compared with the buying power of other groups. According to a 2018 study by the University of Georgia, U.S. total estimated buying power was approximately $14.8 trillion, of which white Americans comprised $12.1 trillion, which is a much larger number than $1.3 trillion. In the case of net worth, the predicted $0 median net worth of Blacks is relevant because the median wealth of white American families is predicted to climb to $137,000 over the same period. Did someone say context?

Second—and more important—*income* alone does not translate to *wealth*. In fact, income isn't considered when calculating net worth. Only income applied well, invested, and allowed to compound creates wealth and, over time, impacts one's net worth. Two people making the same amount of money (income) can spend or save so differently that their wealth may differ by seven or more figures (net worth).

If the far-too-often-quoted mythic "buying power" statistic proves anything, it's that if you don't give income a purpose, someone else will, and it won't always make *you* wealthy.

## The Four Purposes of Income

If you work a traditional job where you exchange your time for wages, your income is the single best tool at your disposal to buy the things you need and occasionally purchase things you want. Income is also the primary tool used to prepare for retirement or the point you're unable to work. Consequently, a portion of our income *must* be spent on our needs today and another portion spent on our anticipated future needs. Naturally, the question you may be asking is, "So how much? What percentage of my income should I be spending today versus saving for tomorrow?" Hold your horses. Before we get into numbers, we want to refocus your attention on the approach.

There are *four* purposes of income, organized in sequential phases: security, flexibility, independence, and freedom. Similar to Maslow's hierarchy of needs, the ultimate goal is to have all four purposes achieved simultaneously. The sequential

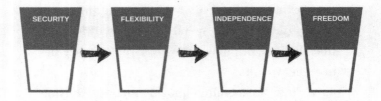

order is important because, typically, only after one purpose is fully met can you proceed to the next. Security must be fully achieved before you can move on to flexibility, flexibility must be fully achieved before you can move on to independence, and so on, until you've reached the ultimate goal of fulfilling all four purposes. This doesn't mean the latter phases should be completely ignored until you're able to work on them, but putting them in this specific order guides your spending decisions along the way.

## 1 | *Security*

The ultimate purpose of income is freedom, and it starts with having a basic sense of security. The money you earn must be enough to cover your physical safety and survival needs. This includes shelter, food, clothing, health care, and all the costs that come with being a healthy, functioning human being. It's also important to note there is no spectrum within this phase. Put another way, you can't be a little bit secure. Either you are financially secure, or you're not. Either you have what you need, or you don't.

*You can't be a little bit secure. Either you are financially secure, or you're not. Either you have enough of what you need, or you don't.*

Being financially secure means your immediate needs are met, but it doesn't mean you have the nicest version of these needs. It simply means your days and decisions aren't burdened by the inability to acquire resources. You have enough to get by and aren't at immediate risk of financial catastrophe. It's also important to note that any money spent in this stage is not working for you. You're working for it.

We've found that reducing spending on the Big 3—housing, transportation, and food—offers the biggest bang for your buck in this phase. That means potentially downsizing, relocating to a more affordable area, sharing a home, or taking advantage of creative mortgage refinancing opportunities available for those who qualify and can afford to take that path. It could also include sharing a car, selling a car, or driving older cars. Last, it means cooking at home as often as possible.

There's a tendency for those in the Middle to disregard or downplay the importance of focusing on the Big 3. This is because people in the Middle have dedicated huge parts of their life to working toward and in anticipation of living in their dream home, driving their dream car, and eating out as

# THE REALITY OF
# FINANCIAL SECURITY

A few years ago, we were asked to sit on a panel and had the pleasure of meeting an amazing young woman. She was in her twenties, a full-time student who worked at Starbucks and drove for Uber to earn a couple extra dollars to afford expensive medical care for her daughter. While we didn't have a full breakdown of her budget in front of us, we could tell from the desperation in her voice that she was on the brink of financial insecurity and fearful of the path she was on.

She had aspirations to start a business and wanted to learn about our experience as real estate investors because she thought it might be a pathway for her to get out of her predicament. Luckily, years later, she sent us a note on Instagram thanking us for inspiring her that day and letting us know that she'd paid off her debts and started a business as a health and mindfulness coach. We asked her how she came so far in such a short period of time, and her response was simple: "I did a little bit of everything." She found a more affordable apartment, focused on landing a better-paying job instead of juggling multiple part-time jobs, and overcame her discomfort with cooking to stretch her budget even further. We were thrilled to hear from her and happy to know that she'd climbed out of the hole she was in and onto firmer ground. Her story is like those of millions of people in the United States, and unfortunately many don't have such happy endings.

According to the Bureau of Labor Statistics, 63 percent of annual household expenses in the United States was spent on housing, transportation, and food.[3] These categories are widely known as the Big 3 because they consume the largest portion of most household budgets. According to the U.S. census, the median earning for households as of 2019 was $68,703.[4] Knowing this, we can assume that just over $43,000 is spent on the Big 3 expenses on an annual basis for the typical family, leaving only $26,000, or just over $2,000 a month, to cover income taxes, health insurance, utilities, insurance, entertainment, student loan debt, and other expenses. Is it any wonder why so many Americans are struggling to save for retirement? Nevertheless, for those of you who can or will be in a position to do so in the future, it's important to gain clarity on what to do with your income once the basics are met.

often as they want. They simply aren't willing to make these trade-offs to get ahead, because their identities are so tied to their belongings and access to the finer things. We're here to tell you that unless you have a proven, consistent, and un-canny ability to earn income at a high level, ignoring these three categories will be a primary contributor to your inability to make financial progress in your life. The sooner you can learn to live on less, the sooner you'll be able to redirect your income to fulfilling other, more meaningful purposes.

Of course, focusing on earning more money is another way to solve for a shortage and can be more sustainable for certain people. Opportunities exist to save in smaller budget catego-ries as well. But by taking a full-scale approach to reducing expenses, you can optimize your income from all angles.

## 2 | *Flexibility*

Once you have achieved financial security, you can begin to fulfill the second purpose of income: flexibility. At this point, you have a small surplus of earnings, and you can decide how to spend it in different ways *without* putting yourself at risk of not covering your essentials.

For example, you could revisit the basics and choose to spend more in those respective categories. You might decide to move out of your current living space and find a better, slightly more expensive home. Or you might choose to buy a newer car or shop at a better grocery store. All of these op-tions are available, and that's what makes this particular stage tricky.

It's easy for people with growing incomes to achieve pur-pose one (security) and then get stuck in purpose two (flexi-bility). Remember what we told you about the Middle? Many of them have deep memories of what it's like to be financially insecure, and their taste preferences are largely shaped by the Fast Spenders. So naturally, as soon as they have the option to splurge a little bit, they take full advantage of it. Who can blame them? Everyone deserves a reward for their hard work, especially if they've waited a long time for it. The problem is, once the genie's out of the bottle, it's really hard to put it back in. They become victims of what is known as "lifestyle inflation," the tendency to counteract an increase in income with corresponding increases in spending.

This is why car dealerships are so flexible in allowing you to test-drive a car or take it home for the weekend. This is why real estate agents show you homes that match your search criteria and one that's just a notch above your budget. And this is why banks are more than willing to offer you multiple options for taking out a loan. They know that when given the choice, most people will opt to continue enjoying the short-term comforts of flexibility even if it puts their long-term goals at risk.

Before we go any further, it's important to call this out: we don't stand for shaming people for their buying preferences. We are not cut from the same cloth as those who ridicule our community for desiring and purchasing nice things. Shame is a poor motivator, so we have no interest in adding to the finger-pointing so many of us already experience from media pundits and out-of-touch personal finance gurus. It's our job to provide you with perspective so that you're aware of alternatives and can sharpen your decision-making process.

Some people who could achieve all four purposes of

income decide to, once they've accomplished one, forgo the others. That's their decision.

But there will come a point where you'll have to transition from just working for your money to allowing your money to work for you. Flexibility is the first test of your leadership skills.

When you spend your money, it's gone forever, but when you invest your money, you're giving it an opportunity to grow. As your money grows, it has the potential to produce future income for you. You won't always have the energy or capability to actively earn income, so by "employing" your income today, you are ensuring you have money you can rely on in the future. It's worth reiterating that most people in the Middle understand this concept in theory but struggle with abiding by it for three reasons:

1 | They assume they will always be able to earn income at the same level or more in the future.
2 | They overestimate employment stability and their desire to work.
3 | They fail to prepare for unexpected occurrences outside of work that impact their spending.

In other words, they are blindly optimistic (another signature American characteristic). Don't believe us? Just ask someone how they're doing and wait for the automated response—"good!" Americans are so optimistic that it's socially frowned upon to answer that question honestly. In the face of social unrest, a plunging stock market, the threat of climate change, and sickness, the typical American will almost certainly mask the negativity with a sunny perspective. This optimism and short-term thinking lures us to borrow from our future and blocks us from employing the life-changing power of "enough."

Again, there are clearly other factors for why so many people find themselves stuck in the Middle with no clear path toward a healthy retirement: the rising cost of living, flat wage growth, financial illiteracy, aggressive sales tactics, and predatory lending, among others. But in this book, we're choosing to focus primarily on the behaviors and mindsets we have immediate control over. The fact remains that if we spend all of our surplus income on short-term wants and needs, there won't be enough to save or invest for our future needs. If you want to move on to eventual financial freedom and cash out, you have to progress *past* this stage and onto the next purpose.

Making the mindset shift from seeing your income as fruit you can enjoy today to seeing your income as seeds to be planted for tomorrow is critical for retirement planning and fulfilling the next purpose of income.

## DEFINING ENOUGH

Look no further than the storage industry for evidence of America's addiction to excess. According to *Forbes*, $241 million was spent on mini storage facility construction in 2011.[5] By 2018, that number had increased to $5 billion with units regularly maintaining 90 percent occupancy rates. This is on top of the 16 percent increase in average home square footage between 2000 and 2018, according to Statista.[6] So even with the steadily increasing size of homes, garages, closets, and basements, Americans still don't have enough space to store all the stuff they buy.

The author Ronald Wright describes this phenomenon as the "progress trap."[7] His theory is that people pursue what they think is progress and initially solve a short-term problem, only to also create a long-term threat that they don't have the resources to solve.

The flexibility phase was where we really examined our relationship with things. Instead of letting our home get full of "stuff" without thinking about what we buy, why we bought it, how we'll use it, and how we'll store it, we stopped, asked questions, and became very intentional. We traded up on the things that mattered but realized there were a lot of things we could still enjoy without owning them. Instead of buying a fancier espresso machine, we chose to visit our local coffee shop a few times a month. Instead of buying books, we opted to borrow them from libraries. Instead of buying a huge cable package, we simply bought the shows we wanted to watch and rented the rest. The question wasn't about whether we could afford these items. It was about whether the purchase was worth it compared with what we knew our money could do for us in the future.

Instead of looking at money as an infinite access to "things," look at it as the mechanism you can use to gain all four purposes, not just one or two. Again, as we discussed in the opening chapter, you are your own solution. You have to make the decision to remedy your own circumstances and progress to another purpose, if you so wish. If you choose otherwise, that's your decision, and everyone should respect it. We certainly do.

## 3 | *Independence*

The third purpose of income is to achieve independence. At this point, going to work to earn more money is completely optional. You will have already saved and invested enough money or built enough passive income to support your lifestyle.

It's easy to assume this stage of life is reserved only for the super-rich, but with the growth of the financial independence movement online and a historic bull market beginning in 2009, more working- and middle-class people are achieving this feat every single day. But to get there, you will have to make a fundamental shift in your relationship with and understanding of income. You must believe your income can work harder than you can. Instead of working for your money, you must adjust to managing your money so that it can multiply over time to serve your future wants and needs. If you choose to continue working, despite not needing the income, your approach to that work will change as a result of your independence.

Have you ever wondered what work you would do if you didn't need the money? Well, financially independent people go beyond just thinking about how to answer that question; they actually pursue it.

If this still feels far-fetched to you, we have good news. There are three levels to financial independence you should know.

**Low independence:** This is also known as Coast or Barista FI. If you've achieved low independence, you have invested enough in a retirement account and don't need to make future contributions. You've already calculated how much you need to retire and can safely assume the money you have will grow into your target amount in the future. Because you no longer need to add funds to your traditional retirement, you can opt to take on less stressful part-time work as needed just to cover your monthly expenses or to receive employer-sponsored benefits like health care, without disrupting the growth in your accounts.

**Mid-independence:** This is the most traditional form of financial independence and is achieved when you have an investment portfolio that is a minimum of twenty-five times your annual spending. At this point, not only have you saved enough for retirement, but you don't have to earn income at all because you can safely withdraw and live off the interest earned from your investments. The amount you withdraw can vary but is predominantly based on what is known as the 4 percent rule, which states that a well-balanced and efficient investment portfolio can be drawn down from at an annual rate of 4 percent with little risk of ever reaching $0. In theory, because the growth of the portfolio exceeds the withdrawal and rate of inflation, the portfolio will maintain a positive balance for the foreseeable future.

**High independence:** This is also known as Fat FIRE and is reached when you have significantly more than twenty-five times your annual spending. You may still abide by the 4 percent rule, but you can easily spend more than that without concern or feeling the need to replace the income. People who are financially independent typically aim for mid-independence and walk away from their jobs as soon as they hit their target number. But if you have higher aspirations and don't want to be bound by the limitations of the 4 percent rule, aim for even higher investment portfolio balances.

Achieving any degree of financial independence is an incredible accomplishment and provides you with a level of security most people only dream of. Depending on your level, it may not be the ultra-luxurious life of the rich and famous we see on television and movie screens, but you can go to sleep at night knowing you will always have enough, which for most people is a dream come true.

## SEED MONEY

Let's assume ten years ago you were paid in seeds, not money. With every payday you were given a bag of seeds, which you could eat or plant for future harvest. If you planted 5 to 10 percent of your seeds, after ten years you'd have a garden you would be proud of but likely not enough to feed you for the foreseeable future. But if you were able to consistently plant upward of 50 or 70 percent of those seeds, after ten years you wouldn't have a small garden; you'd have an orchard. In fact, you might have so many fruits and vegetables you won't know what to do with them. Sure, you might eat some, but you'd have so much excess you'd likely give some away to neighbors and others in your community. The same thing can happen with your income through the power of compounding interest. We won't get into the detailed tactics here. That comes a little later in chapter 7. But the idea is simple: money is fertile and has the potential to grow far beyond its present value.

Most people in the Middle understand this concept as well, but still haven't made the commitment to aggressively plant their seeds. This is partly due to the lack of relatable role models who offer a clear and tangible example of what life may look like if different financial decisions were made. Instead of fearing the Financially Insecure life or drooling over the Fast Spender life, surround yourself with more like-minded people who are actively pursuing financial independence.

The time we've spent with and around financially independent people has been incredibly valuable. Some of them have achieved this degree of liberty through years of employing frugality and consistently investing in the stock market. Others have spent years in real estate or growing online businesses that they've sold or handed off to a manager to take care of the day-to-day activities. With their independence, many have gone on to pursue a life of activism, politics, or entrepreneurial ventures with a social aspect. Any approach is fine, but what is consistent in every approach is steady, focused effort and a deep appreciation of time. Because they aren't forced to exchange their time for money, time itself becomes the most valuable resource they have, and they protect it at all costs.

## 4 | *Freedom*

The fourth and final purpose of income is freedom. There are two things about freedom you should know.

"Freedom" is one of those words you could spend a lifetime trying to fully understand because it's so amorphous. While it's a universally accepted term, freedom means different things to everyone. For the Financially Insecure, freedom could simply be getting a better job, moving out of a neighborhood, or having a financial obligation removed. If you're a Fast Spender, freedom could be a state of emotional acceptance, closing a big deal, or selling a company you've built from the ground up. But for the Middle—once again—freedom tends to be a bit more difficult to envision.

Similar to the Middle's struggle to identify how much is enough, freedom is an ever-changing milestone that always seems just out of reach. We know several people who've successfully achieved financial independence but failed at earning financial freedom. Instead, they continue working, telling themselves, *Just another year* or *I'm waiting to get fired to collect a fat severance package.* If nothing else, their responses illustrate a profound truth: financial freedom isn't a number; it's a feeling.

We sensed our version of freedom on our honeymoon, even though it was for only two weeks. During our honeymoon, the feeling we had after spending time away from the office, work culture, and the American media machine intoxicated us. During our time in South Africa, we were also free from the self-induced pressure we'd placed on ourselves to uphold the image of Black excellence. While we certainly had luxury experiences, most of our treasured moments were not expensive at all. Experiences like trying a $20 bottle of South

African wine we'd never heard of before, savoring $10 barbecue in Soweto (what they call a *braai*), and leaving generous cash tips for the waitstaff are what made our time there unforgettable. We'd paid for our honeymoon in full, far in advance of taking it, and in doing so gave ourselves a taste of our future life.

Even that small precursor of freedom afforded us time to get to know ourselves as individuals and reintroduce each other to the people we once were. We held hands and sustained eye contact during introspective conversations. We asked taxi drivers to pull over as we took time to explore corners of Cape Town on foot. We strolled through museums and neighborhoods, read books, took pictures, and healed from the remarkable damage we'd done to our bodies. We thought about our local community and how we might be able to use the skills we'd acquired over the years to do more than make our then employer richer.

That trip embodied *our* definition of freedom. And, while we hadn't fully achieved this purpose in a permanent way yet, we knew that our future freedom needed to feel *exactly* like that trip.

For you, freedom may be granting yourself permission to break up with a career, walk away from an abusive relationship, or enter long-term rehabilitation or therapy. For the millions of people who are financially responsible for aging parents in addition to their own children, freedom may be taking months off from work or leaving a job altogether so you can organize your family's finances and end the cycle of multigenerational poverty. Whatever it is, it's usually deeply personal and almost impossible to place an exact dollar figure on.

### FREEDOM IS NEVER GIVEN. IT'S TAKEN.

Credit card companies, banks, and medical, financial, and government institutions do not willingly offer or grant freedom from debts owed to them. That freedom is either earned, taken, or paid for. And when you are a prisoner of your own making, chaining yourself to beliefs, obligations, or lofty utopian goals, only *you* can release yourself from the social and cultural contracts you've signed. As much as this deep internal work requires emotional strength, your income is one of the most powerful tools you can use, starting with carving out the time to develop a plan with this newfound purpose in mind. It can give you a moment to breathe, think, and reassess the trajectory you're on—to determine whether you like the person you are today or the person you're becoming.

No one's going to give you financial freedom. If you want it, you're going to need to take it.

EVERY TIME YOU ACHIEVE one purpose and start to move on to the next, your relationship with income shifts. And just as you might anticipate having to learn different skills as you transition into a leadership position at your job, you'll need to be prepared to lead and manage your money so that it works hard on your behalf.

When it comes to managing money, it's common for you to feel a full range of emotions, particularly angst and worry.

Oftentimes, at the root of those feelings is confusion about how much to save, whether you're making the right investment decisions, or how to navigate competing financial priorities. This is why the purpose of income framework is so important to help guide you through the decision-making process and remind you of what's at stake when you're faced with a financial decision. You may even think of it as a financial compass so that wherever you are along your journey, you can rely on this as a trusted guide to help point you in the right direction.

## rules

*On spending and saving:*

- Avoid the progress trap. Learning to live below your means, even as you earn more money, is key to ultimately achieving financial freedom.
- You can't manage what you don't measure. So, at minimum, you should be monitoring your spending on a monthly basis. As you develop this discipline, you can opt to do this less frequently and informally—but never take your eye off the ball.
- Focus on reducing spending in the Big 3 first (housing, transportation, and food) to make the largest impact on your savings goals.

*On earning:*

- There is only so much you can save. At some point, to achieve your savings goals, you'll need to focus on earning more, particularly if your plan is to build considerable wealth. We discuss more about income in detail in chapter 6.

# richuals

- **Before you upgrade or spend more on something, apply 80/20 thinking.** For example, if purchasing a more expensive car will bring you disproportionally greater joy, then feel free to make the purchase, assuming it's within your budget. Costly purchases that don't bring you disproportionate joy are indicators that you may be prioritizing status or trendiness over independence and freedom.

- **Instead of asking yourself "can I afford it?" ask yourself "at what cost?"** Habitually making short-term sacrifices for long-term gain can be challenging. To help ease the discomfort, you must remind yourself of what you're gaining from the decision and what could be lost in the future if you choose to spend more today.

*Note: For more information on reducing spending, check out the appendix, "Some Tips on Saving," and for more tools and resources, check our website richandregular.com/resources*

# CHAPTER 4

# The Fifteen-Year Career

Most people never really think about how long their careers should be. Rather, they hope for a long and successful one, and power through until retirement or, well, death. But how long is long? How do you determine whether your career was successful? And why would we willingly repeat the mistakes of previous generations when the outcome is clearly unfavorable?

It is our belief that you should plan for your career to be fifteen years long. That's it.

Now, does that mean that after graduating from college and landing a first real job at twenty-two, everyone should be in a position to retire at thirty-seven? Of course not. We understand the litany of factors that can influence one's income, health, living expenses, and portfolio returns over a fifteen-year horizon. But if you're interested in pursuing a financially independent life, fifteen years is a solid target.

Think about it. We all generally accept that a focused

four-year college education is plenty of time to have developed a fundamental mastery of a discipline. It's enough to earn a decent wage and begin a career with a fair chance of success. Similarly, in terms of relationships, we generally understand that a five-year relationship is considered a serious one and that ten is damn near forever. The phrase seven-year itch was coined in the 1950s because right around the seventh year of marriage and particularly after having raised their first child, couples tend to know whether they're going to make it or not. According to a 2014 *Vox* article about the typical American life, "The average length of a US marriage that ends in divorce is about seven years. Remarkably, federal data shows this has been the case since as far back as 1867."[1]

So if a four-year education is enough to have a fundamental understanding of a subject and a ten-year relationship is an eternity, then a fifteen-year career is a pretty long one. Come to think of it, fifteen years of doing anything is long, and it's certainly long enough to project future outcomes. And at the end of the day, the math works the same whether it's the career you have from age forty-five to sixty or from twenty-two to thirty-seven.

Before we go any further, we should mention two caveats. First, it's much easier to do this if you're in a dual-income household with both adults receiving above-average incomes. It's even easier if you're a dual-income household without children or other dependents. Obviously, dual-income households benefit from multiple income sources, twice as many opportunities for advancement, shared responsibilities at home, and tax benefits, if married, compared with single people. Second, when we talk about a fifteen-year career, we are primarily referring to the careers of college-educated and/or upwardly mobile workers with specialized skills. The notion of doing this as a low-wage worker is practically impossible, especially if you have children.

But if your professional career is already in motion, you're earning a decent income, and you agree with our four purposes of income framework, then your next step is to start planning your career with a definitive exit plan. It's time to start designing a life that slowly and increasingly gives you power, instead of one that drains you of it.

So if you're ready, let's dive in.

## Years 1–5: Pay Off Debt

For many millennials, early adulthood and the beginning phases of their careers can be defined by one word: "debt." It's a pervasive cloud over an entire generation's head as they combated both the crippling 2008 economic downturn and a soaring rise in the cost of higher education. For Black women especially, there's immense pride in being the leading recipients of associate and bachelor's degrees conferred as of 2016.[2] Unfortunately, the achievement is smothered by the harsh reality of student loans. According to a 2020 *Business Insider* article, the average student loan debt balance of Black students was just over $32,000, more than twice that of Hispanic students and over 40 percent higher than white students.[3] This means that upon graduation, on average, Black students (mostly women) are already in a deep hole that is made even more difficult to climb out of due to pay disparities in the workplace.

We could go into intense detail about the gender and racial pay gap, predatory lending practices, and how many proposals have been floated to provide relief to this generation's student loan debt crisis. We could be optimistic and continue to wait for the government to intervene on a large scale, which as of the time we're writing this book hasn't happened. Or we can decide that we're done waiting. As we've said several times before, there comes a time when we must recognize the urgency of a situation and do what we know must be done. Extreme times call for extreme measures and extreme language.

Take an issue as pervasive as homelessness for example. Unfortunately, it's socially acceptable to ignore unhoused people or worse: judge them for some type of moral failure. But homelessness isn't always caused by a moral failure. A 2015 study by the National Law Center on Homelessness and Poverty revealed that among the leading causes of homelessness are insufficient income, unemployment, mental illness, lack of affordable housing, and domestic violence.[4] In 2021, a different study, entitled "Reality Check: Paycheck-to-Paycheck," was conducted and revealed that nearly 40 percent of Americans with annual income over $100,000 live paycheck to paycheck.[5]

Think about those two statistics for a moment. Most people can only dream of making $100,000 a year. Yet today that's still not enough money to keep a significant portion of the U.S. population from living on the edge. This perpetual state of living paycheck to paycheck leads to debt. And as that debt grows, so does the pressure to maintain appearances, health and wellness standards, and any semblance of a fulfilling life until eventually you can't afford a home anymore. We don't expect you to envision your future self as homeless someday, but you owe it to yourself to measure just how far from the edge you are and how quickly your situation could spiral out of control.

Personal debt should be viewed the same way you would view an invasive cancer in your life. In general, when people we know receive a cancer diagnosis, there's an unwavering seriousness. They shift their entire life around to fight the disease, and the people in their corner offer their full support. With that energy in mind, we've found the single best way to eliminate debt is to take a holistic and community-based approach to aggressively paying it off. This means that for the first five years of your fifteen-year career, assuming you have debt, you need to make frugality a core aspect of your life. Your primary objective should be an intense focus on paying down your debt entirely or at least reducing it to a manageable level. Every increase in pay, income tax refund, gift, and coin hidden in your couch is an opportunity to funnel money toward paying down your debt.

There are a number of ways people have done this, but the right strategy for someone else might not be the right one for you. If freezing your credit cards in blocks of ice and living a cash-only life knocks out your car payment, then it doesn't matter if someone you trust recommends a totally different approach. Try them all on for size, but double down on the ones that best fit your lifestyle and enable you to reduce what you owe. During our debt-payoff years, we used the avalanche method and snowball method.

## *The Avalanche Method*

The avalanche method is an approach to debt elimination that involves paying off debts that have the highest interest rate first. When those balances are paid off, you then move on to the debts with the next-highest interest rates until all debts are paid. This can be a slow, painful grind, but it ensures you've paid the least amount of interest to creditors.

For instance, let's assume you had two credit cards: a Visa with a balance of $15,000 and a Mastercard with a $10,000 balance. Now let's say the Visa has an interest rate (or APR) of 15 percent while the Mastercard has an interest rate of 10 percent. Using the avalanche method, you'd focus your attention on paying down the Visa because it's accumulating interest on a revolving basis at a higher interest rate than the other card. You'll still pay the minimum balance on the Mastercard to avoid additional fees, but the surplus income you have will go toward paying off the Visa in full. Once the Visa's outstanding balance is paid down, you'd repeat the process by focusing on paying off the Mastercard. By using this approach, you ensure you pay the least amount of money in total.

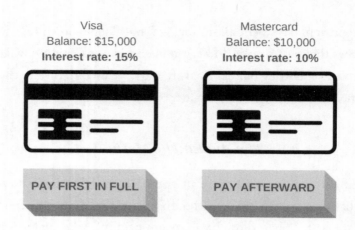

Visa
Balance: $15,000
**Interest rate: 15%**

Mastercard
Balance: $10,000
**Interest rate: 10%**

**PAY FIRST IN FULL**

**PAY AFTERWARD**

### *The Snowball Method*

With the snowball method, instead of attacking debts with the highest interest rates, you'd pay off the debts with the smallest balances first. For example, let's say your Mastercard has a balance of $5,000 and an interest rate of 10 percent. Now let's assume your Visa has a balance of $7,000 and an interest rate of 15 percent. This time, you'd allocate your surplus dollars to paying off the Mastercard first, even though it has a higher interest rate than the Visa. Don't worry, there is a method to this madness.

Research shows that for many people the snowball approach has the tendency to feel more rewarding because you shrink the number of creditors you owe earlier in the process. In this case, you had only two credit cards with outstanding balances. But if you had five, the research suggests there is a greater likelihood of overall success when you can quickly reduce the number of creditors you owe. With that positive momentum on your side, there's a tendency to be more motivated

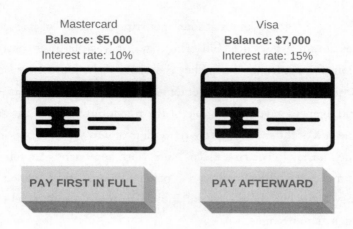

| Mastercard | Visa |
| --- | --- |
| **Balance: $5,000** | **Balance: $7,000** |
| Interest rate: 10% | Interest rate: 15% |
| PAY FIRST IN FULL | PAY AFTERWARD |

throughout the journey, making you more likely to pay down your debts.

## Don't Forget to Reward Yourself

We've accomplished a lot in our lives, both together and individually, but there were few things more difficult than the early years of debt payoff as a couple. It's the reason we call budgeting the financial equivalent of burpees. If you've ever tried to lose weight or get back in shape after allowing your health and fitness to flounder, then you know the feeling we're referring to. Just as you will have cravings for a slice of pizza after a long week of cardio, you will have urges to spend money on things that don't contribute to your debt-payoff goals while living frugally. In those moments, we can't express how important it is to carve out bite-size moments of pleasure so that you can scratch that itch.

For us, it was splurging on a nice meal at home to get the

feeling of going out without incurring the cost of a nice restaurant experience. On other days, it was planning vacations far in advance during key moments of the year where we anticipated we'd be in desperate need of a break. These mini-indulgences gave us a sample of the freedom we knew was at the end of the road and were reminders of why we'd set out on the journey in the first place. Note, both approaches are relevant for debts like credit cards, personal loans, and home equity loans but should not be applied to more complex debts such as mortgages.

## rules

*Years 1–5:*

- **Frugality isn't an f-word.** The word "frugal" often has a negative connotation. It has been associated with words like "cheap," "stingy," or "frumpy." Instead, you should embrace the term, just as you do noble characteristics like loyalty, responsibility, and intentionality.

- **Debt payoff is a raise.** Whenever you eliminate a debt, in essence you're increasing the amount of surplus cash you have on hand. The ability to do this early in your career is an act of self-empowerment, and financially akin to giving yourself a promotion. You don't have to wait. If you deserve a raise now, give yourself one.

# Years 6–10: Find Your Superpower

Focusing on paying off debt in the first five years of your career also has a surprising effect on your career choices. Before we started paying off our debt, earning potential was the single most important factor in the kinds of jobs we considered. We'd spend hours scrolling through job descriptions and drooling over salary ranges as we imagined what our lives would be like bringing home those paychecks. But as we started to pay off debts and our monthly cost of living decreased, we found ourselves less intrigued by job openings simply because they paid more than we were making. Earning an extra few hundred dollars a month suddenly didn't seem worth it, because we'd already proven we could accomplish the same financial goal by paying down a debt.

So instead of chasing money or a title, we chased the challenge. The way we approached goal setting became less about what roles paid us more in the short run and more about what skills we could develop to support us in the long run—far beyond the length of time we were reliant on others for employment.

When Kendra Barnes was a senior in high school, her mother told her that if Kendra got a full-ride scholarship to college, she'd buy her a car. That was all Kendra needed to hear to study hard, search for, and ultimately earn a scholarship to North Carolina A&T State University, a historically Black college. Kendra ultimately graduated with a degree in agricultural economics and went on to earn a master's degree from Purdue University in the same field.

In 2008, she went on to become an international economist for the U.S. government, analyzing crop production and coordinating food assistance programs. From the outside looking in, you'd be right to assume that she was living the dream. She was highly educated, was earning a good income, had great benefits, and was celebrated as one of the few young Black women at her level. The only problem was, she didn't really enjoy the work.

After a few years, her frustration hit a high point after a conversation with a supervisor. A co-worker two pay grades above her left their job, and Kendra was asked to take on the extra work until a replacement was found. She complied with the request and was even told she was doing a wonderful job in the interim. When the job opening was announced, Kendra told her supervisor that she was interested in the role but was told she was too young—that her co-workers, most of whom were twenty years her senior, were more deserving of the role because they'd been there longer. "You need to pay your dues," her supervisor said. Coming out of college, Kendra was specifically recruited into the department as part of the National Scholars Program. Now that she was there and performing well, she was being held back from a pay increase for a job she was already doing.

Kendra could've accepted her supervisor's direction and waited. She could've opted to find another department or rebuild her career in another government agency. But instead

Kendra took control of her career trajectory outside her job to get the raise she was looking for. She used the data analysis, communication, and coordination skills she'd honed in her job to tackle the world of real estate investing, and she hasn't looked back since.

In 2013, Kendra purchased her first rental property. Over the next few years, she'd acquire six more rental units, and soon the money she earned from her real estate portfolio exceeded what she was making in her job. Finally, at the age of thirty-two, Kendra cashed out. Her career in government lasted eleven years, and today, as a retired real estate investor, she spends her days with her family and helping others replicate her real estate success through her website, thekeyresource.com.

Once you've paid off your debt, the next five years of your career should be dedicated to creating multiple income streams, or an income portfolio, outside your primary job. As Kendra discovered, at some point most of us will brush up against barriers at work, whether it's unfair hiring practices or inconvenient layoffs that prevent us from moving up and making more money. The bottom line is that we can't depend on our jobs alone to give us what we need or want. Your approach to creating an income portfolio can look like participating in the gig economy, starting your own business, or even investing in real estate as Kendra did. We'll go in depth into some of the approaches in chapter 6, but for now we want to focus on one of the best and most popular ways to create income: real estate. Next to investments in the stock market, real estate has played a significant role in creating most of the world's millionaires.

## *Real Estate*

Real estate is one of the best ways to utilize almost any super-power: your superpower could be sales skills that allow you to find prospective buyers quickly, or it could be your ability to fix things, which makes managing repairs a breeze. For others, it could be your skills as a team leader that make managing multiple contractors, mortgage lenders, buyers, and sellers easy. Whatever it is, there's a pretty good chance you already have transferable skills that will help you make the transition into real estate.

What makes stories like Kendra's so amazing isn't just that she built a real estate portfolio that outearned her job, or even that she was able to walk away from her job at the age of thirty-two. It's that Kendra found and exploited her superpower outside work. She could've done what well-meaning and well-respected advisers suggested and waited her turn for a promotion. But she wanted more for herself and took full control of her earning potential despite not being an expert, breaking a few trusted rules of thumb along the way.

Also, she didn't have all the answers or do everything right when she started in real estate. Going against traditional personal finance rules of thumb, she took a loan from her retirement account to buy her first property. When she got the duplex, it already had a tenant, and Kendra didn't even know to ask for a copy of the lease agreement to understand the terms. Nevertheless, she found the resolve to figure it out and the willingness to hang on throughout the process.

Kendra embodies the spirit of betting on yourself and not

allowing anyone else to determine your worth. Kendra really did cash out. "Before you get into real estate investing, it feels like you have to be wealthy before getting started. But once you get into it, you feel, oh . . . I can do this. Then it's like . . . look at how much money we're making. Let's do it again," said Kendra.

## OUR REAL ESTATE STORY

When we purchased our first rental five years into our corporate careers, it didn't meet the coveted 1 percent rule of rental real estate investing.[6] Additionally, we didn't have cash reserves to cover unexpected expenses and were still undecided as to whether we'd secure a third party to manage the property or do it ourselves. What we did know is that we had good credit and consistent income. If we needed to cover the mortgage payments on the property, we had options to do so while we figured it all out.

Like Kendra, we found confidence in the business, management, and analytical skills we'd developed at our day jobs. We knew we'd have to negotiate with contractors, potential tenants, and sellers and felt comfortable doing it outside work because we'd done it so many times in our jobs. Whenever we traveled on business, we made a point to review property values in other cities because it gave us anecdotal and comparative evidence to support our decisions. Last, we took it upon ourselves to review company data, reports, and other sources of information that served as indicators of the general health of the lending market. This helped us consider whether it was the right time to apply for a secondary mortgage. None of this was directly tied to the jobs we had or the departments we worked for. But as employees of a large company, we absorbed the information available to us and applied it to our lives outside work.

Looking back, if we had to point to just one thing that helped us as successful real estate investors, it would have very little to do with our natural-born intellect or academic achievement. No, what made our real estate investing experience a successful one was the fact that we could manage the cost of ownership if needed. Our ability to comfortably carry the second mortgage was a greater contributor to our success than our ability to find properties and analyze deals. And this wouldn't have been possible had we not spent the early part of our careers living frugally to pay down debt. If we'd chosen to move into a larger home and purchase new vehicles instead, we wouldn't have had the surplus cash to make a down payment, and our creditworthiness would've been less attractive to lenders.

Finding and honing a niche can be the spark you need to eventually earn your way out of a job. As you try to climb in your career, you will undoubtedly hit some roadblocks, and it may be tempting to take them personally. Quite frankly, you may be well within your right to feel that way. But don't let feeling slighted overshadow the larger mission. Instead, funnel that frustration into something productive, something that appreciates in value, something that will eventually free you.

# rules

*Years 6–10:*

- **Open an investment account that isn't tied to your employer.** Investing is so intertwined with employment that we forget there are other options. We unpack this more in chapter 7, but, generally, at this stage, you should open a taxable brokerage account outside your employer-directed retirement accounts. This will allow you to access your money prior to retirement age without penalty. Assuming you have a fully funded emergency fund, you should begin investing in this account as often as possible.

- **Confident people get hired first.** Use this phase of your career to invest in your skills and network to increase the value you bring to the table. If you're unsure of what you're good at, listen to how others talk about you and solicit unbiased feedback regularly. When you know what your strengths are and how they're valued in the marketplace, you become a much better negotiator.

- **Leave a memorable footprint.** Social platforms like LinkedIn have changed the way recruiters and other influential people find talent. It's important that they know who you are well before you need something from them (and vice versa). Begin to share your strengths and wins publicly because closed mouths don't get fed.
- **The value of income is relative.** You must gain the ability to compare income you've earned on your own to income earned from an employer. This enables you to put employer feedback and their projected growth plan for your career into perspective. An income source can be considered a quality income source only if you have something else to compare it to.

## Years 11–15: Build an Escape Hatch

Congratulations! You've just worked for an entire decade, and assuming it's with the same company, you may have the option of choosing a gift from their online store. But don't get your hopes up. Instead of a trip to Hawaii or a Rolex watch, you'll have your choice of a crystal paperweight, a leaf blower, or a watercooler that's entirely too big and available only in your least favorite color. Let this be your motivation to finish the last five years of your career focused on your departure.

When Purple, the anonymous writer behind the popular blog apurplelife.com, began her professional career, she was well prepared to navigate the political roadblocks she would face. In the 1980s, her mother worked as a chemical engineer and human resources director for a handful of Fortune 500 companies. As one of only a few working, professional Black women during that time, her mother fought through her own set of experiences and managed to retire early at the age of fifty-five. Having seen this example up close, Purple was well primed to deal with workplace dynamics and knew that at a minimum a similar retirement age was possible for her. But after years of savvy job-hopping and frugal living, she very quickly realized she could do it much sooner.

"Watching my mom, she'd already told me what was going to happen," Purple told us. "Your boss is gonna come in; they're going to pay you a little bit and make you do everything. Seeing and hearing her distaste for it . . . I went in knowing that a long career wouldn't make me happy."

Even when she landed what she thought was her dream job—working in advertising in New York City—the sense of fulfillment was short-lived. During her mom's working years, there were clear boundaries; people worked from 9:00 a.m. to 5:00 p.m. But Purple's work demands were different. She was expected to respond to texts and emails on her company-provided mobile phone and laptop at all times. She was required to be on conference calls for her global clients sometimes as early as one in the morning. Even after doing this and hitting all her performance metrics, she was refused a promotion and told by her senior VP, "You're not ready."

Discouraged and disillusioned, Purple decided to play the game to her advantage. Instead of staying in a particular role or with a company under the assumption that her hard work and loyalty would eventually be rewarded, she changed her approach. "I job hopped. For a while, I moved every year, and with almost every move I'd earn another $20,000. Why would I stay in one role doing the same work when someone else that I've only known for an hour in an interview is telling me they'll pay me more to do it for them?" Purple told us.

But that wasn't all. After stumbling across the FIRE movement, Purple began to embrace a frugal lifestyle. The combination of earning higher income, reducing her cost of living, and investing her money in index funds enabled her to make some serious financial gains.

At the start of her career, in 2011, her net worth was $5,000. By 2015, after reevaluating her lifestyle and spending, it ballooned to just under $90,000. Intrigued by the momentum, she began to share her story to connect and learn from others and to help hold herself accountable for her financial goals. In doing so, she has been able to keep her spending under $20,000 for several consecutive years through savvy credit card hacking, cooking at home, and rejecting the mindless consumerism that had once defined her life. By October 2020, with a net worth of more than $530,000, Purple officially achieved financial independence. Even after she quit, as the stock market continued to boom in 2020, her net worth grew to $738,000 by October 2021. Altogether, her working career was a short nine years.

No longer reliant on her salary for income, Purple now earns money from the dividends paid from her investment portfolio. Tapping into the creative and marketing skills she developed in her professional career, she also earns a modest, supplementary amount of income from her blog, which she's committed to operating for a few years after her official retirement. Eventually, she'll fully embrace the lazy life, traveling the world and a growing list of hobbies.

We had the pleasure of speaking with Purple's mom (whom we affectionately call Mama Purple) and asked how she felt about her young, rich, and lazy retired daughter. "Didn't you teach her that hard work was a virtue?" we asked her. Laughing and with no hesitation, Mama Purple replied, "What can I say . . . [apparently] she got it from me." She certainly had gotten it from her: unknowingly, her mother's advice had been the very thing that sparked her desire for financial independence!

Purple is the purest example of cashing out we've ever heard. While she didn't take the entrepreneurial, real estate, or side-hustle route, she doubled down on her relentless discipline. Instead of finding or developing the next big idea, she simply poured all of her extra time into minimizing her spending. She was also willing to break social norms and common career advice by routinely job-hopping and effectively used that tactic to grow her income significantly over a focused period of time. All of this enabled her to funnel all discretionary income into her retirement portfolio and reach her target retirement number well ahead of schedule. And while her professional career didn't even last fifteen years, she embodies what the last phase of the fifteen-year career should look like: discipline, trusting the process, and focusing on the things you can control.

If you're like Purple and you don't have a taste for entrepreneurship, then years 11 through 15 are all about repetition. At this point, investing should feel like financial muscle memory. You should have developed a strong budgeting discipline, set ample cash aside for emergencies, and completely eliminated all debt like credit cards and student loans. Your attention should be squarely focused on padding investment accounts.

For most people, this looks like the following:

1 | Maxing out tax-deferred retirement accounts like 401(k)s, 403(b)s, and IRAs.
2 | Maxing out health savings accounts (HSAs) and investing your contributions (a core benefit to that account).
3 | Contributing targeted amounts to a taxable brokerage account to be used for funding short-term needs.
4 | Funding alternative investment accounts for children and tax benefits like college savings accounts and custodial IRAs.

If you have an itch to be your own boss, the goal is the same, except your focus during years 11–15 should also be on creating the income you need to fund those accounts. This is the time you're putting yourself out there, sharing your ideas with the world, selling and refining your pitch. In the previous five-year stretch, you will have already developed the professional skills you need, understood the business landscape, and determined how you can fill a need. The only thing left to do is to sell something (more on this in chapter 6).

Earning income outside your primary job is one of the

most thrilling experiences you'll ever have. It gives you a completely different set of data to base your efforts on, and over time you'll start to develop a taste preference for income. Specifically, you'll be able to compare the quality of income from your job with the income earned independent of your job. And if you're like Kendra, Purple, or the thousands of side hustlers who've managed to build small fortunes while working, it won't be long before options you didn't know were possible present themselves to you.

## rule

*Years 11–15:*

- **Your title won't be on your tombstone.** In your final years, you'll need to begin the process of decoupling who you are from what you do. The income-earning opportunities available to you as an employee are largely limited by your position. Attracting the wider set of opportunities to create income and shape your legacy requires you to shed labels.

## How to Know When It's Time to Go

One of the best parts of thinking of your career this way is it allows you to get out of debt, develop skills, and pressure test those skills in the marketplace over a fifteen-year stretch. This is why, despite the growing media infatuation with entrepreneurship, we don't go so far as to completely write off the importance of jobs. By and large, well-paying jobs are a good thing and are the primary providers of income for millions of families around the country. But at the same time, jobs are designed to be temporary. Companies have an obligation to innovate, grow revenue, and reduce costs, and history has taught us that this often comes at an inconvenience to workers. The spirit of cashing out is one that recognizes the bigger picture here and ensures you aren't left hanging without the ability to support yourself.

But how do you know when it's time to go? Is there a specific number you should have in your investment accounts or socked away for retirement before giving your notice? As we've said before, the answer to questions like this is oftentimes . . . it depends. In our case, we walked away from one job after having two positive cash-flowing rental properties, having paid off a mortgage, and with years of living on half our household income under our belt. We didn't leave the second job until we'd begun to replace a key portion of our household income as entrepreneurs and had strong indicators of an ability to grow a profitable business.

Let's imagine you've always wanted to take a cross-country trip by car and the vehicle you own has a range of only 350 miles. Yet, at a minimum, you know the full trip is between 5,000 and 7,000 miles round trip. Regardless of the path you've chosen from your home to your final destination, you know there are tons of gas stations along the way. Even if you're driving an electric vehicle, you know there are stations where you can charge your battery sprinkled along your journey. The point is, you don't completely write off the possibility of taking the trip just because you don't have enough gas or battery power for the full journey in the beginning. And you don't pack everything you'll need, because you know there are things you can purchase along the way. The same is true when it comes to determining a specific end date for cashing out. Your accounts may be a little less padded than you'd like, and the stock market may be a little more volatile than you're comfortable with, but it doesn't mean you can't follow your heart and go.

Here are a few questions to ask yourself to help you decide when it's time to quit your job.

## What Kind of Person Is This Job Teaching Me To Be?

If you answer this and discover your job isn't getting in the way of you leading a fulfilling life, then it's perfectly fine to hold on to it and continue padding your investment accounts. In fact, you could alternatively choose to spend significantly more on things that make you happy than you have in previous years. If you don't like the answer to this question, then you should look to cash out sooner rather than later, especially if the job is causing undue stress in your life. There is a reason stress is considered a silent killer, so don't risk ongoing periods of absorbing it simply because you've finished only two-thirds of a marathon.

## Am I Disregarding Other Priorities in My Life That Are Important to Me?

Think about your marriage, children, family, faith, health, or social issues that are important to you. Does your job leave you completely drained with nothing left to give to those areas of your life? If the answer is no, then feel free to extend your stay for as long as you'd like. This implies you have found a healthy balance in your life that allows you to attend to your life's priorities in the way you want. But if the answer is yes, then you should look to cash out sooner rather than later. What good is reaching financial independence if you're spending your newfound freedom in an unhappy home, without the people you care about the most, or in an unhealthy state?

## What Would I Do If the Market Crashed Tomorrow?

One of the benefits of working and investing for more than a decade is that you grow accustomed to the rhythms of the marketplace and the sirens of the financial media. You begin to realize that it's their job to keep your attention and that they'll do it all day without missing a beat. But even if the market did in fact crash the way it did in 2008, and you're only two-thirds of the way through your fifteen-year career, wouldn't you still be in the best financial position possible? You'd be debt-free and have a crystal clear picture of your financial life and years of investments working on your behalf. You'd be one of those people who see downturns as great opportunities to invest more instead of the people too scared to participate. You might have multiple rental properties, investment accounts, or other assets you could sell if needed. The point is, you'd have options most people only dream of having and luckily for you it wouldn't be the end of the world.

## Skeptics, We Hear You

We don't have a crystal ball, but we're pretty sure there will be a small army of skeptics who upon reading our benchmark for a fifteen-year career will say it's absolutely preposterous. They'll say the examples we provided were extreme, that they're outliers and maybe even lucky. Financial analysts and pundits might say that virtually anyone could accomplish what these people did because they were all participants in a historic bull market that saw once-in-a-lifetime gains and skyrocketing real estate values. Some might even say that we and other investors are part of the problem and have contributed to the massive wealth inequality that exists.

This may surprise you, but we encourage you to listen to their perspective, and specifically to what they're not saying. These skeptics are not saying you shouldn't spend a focused period of time paying off debt, or that you shouldn't put yourself in a position to protect your financial well-being by investing heavily in the stock market. They're not saying you shouldn't hustle to develop marketable skills that make you both more employable and more empowered to strike out on your own someday. And they're certainly not celebrating everyday working-class people for spending the entirety of their lives making corporations richer. In fact, the CEOs, entrepreneurs, and media personalities they applaud are often those who have taken unconventional approaches. Isn't that what we're asking you to do?

Perfection isn't the goal here; freedom is. Like we mentioned in chapter 1, chemotherapy is a commonly accepted yet imperfect solution to fighting one of the world's deadliest diseases—cancer. The side effects include hair loss, loss of taste, weight fluctuations, fatigue, and skin discoloration. But when faced with a diagnosis that requires the acceptance of uncomfortable side effects, hundreds of thousands of people a year willingly choose it as the best available option. They do this because they understand the discomfort they'll experience will be temporary and that eventually they'll be able to resume a happier, more fulfilling life.

The same can be said for how you manage the earnings from the first fifteen years of your career. After fifteen years of eliminating debt and steadily investing in appreciating assets, we can assure you, you will have moments of regret. You may miss key moments in your loved ones' lives—join the club of people who've never seen their favorite musician perform live or who've never visited an exotic destination before it was ultimately shut down to tourism. But if you do it well and consistently, at the end of your journey you'll have something that most people in the world don't: the right to choose. You can choose to stay where you are, or you can choose to move on, but no one person or institution will have made the decision for you.

## richuals

- **Choose your boss wisely.** It's widely accepted that people don't leave good companies, they leave bad bosses. Your experience with your manager will shape your experience and career as much as the work itself. If you choose poorly, it could have a lasting effect on your income potential and shape whether or not you're able to achieve your financial goals.

- **Redefine the reward.** Most of us are socialized to view job offers, acceptance, and promotions as the highlights of our careers. These moments serve as status symbols and validating indicators of our intelligence. In truth, jobs should be a means to an end. Your ability to leave a job on your own terms is, in fact, the crowning achievement.

- **The paradox of exposure.** In 1983, the world stood still as Michael Jackson, the greatest pop star of his generation, released his music video for "Thriller." Alongside him, sharing the spotlight for almost every scene of a fourteen-minute video was a young, unknown model, Ms. Ola Ray. The music video and corresponding album would go on to break records around the world, win multiple awards, and earn Jackson millions of dollars. Conversely, Ola was (reportedly) paid $2,500 for her appearance, despite gaining immediate worldwide recognition and being inextricably linked to what is widely considered one of the greatest pop songs of all time. So while exposure can be a perk, it doesn't always convert into income.

## CHAPTER 5

# Freedom Starts in Your Mind

I t was 2013, and we were attending an off-site company meeting. These meetings would typically span consecutive days and served as a crash course on the health of the business. We'd grown to appreciate them because they gave us a chance to meet and collaborate with hundreds of co-workers from around the country. Admittedly, we were most excited for the after-parties because they gave us a chance to truly get to know the people we worked with. Also, if we're being completely honest, these parties presented opportunities to rub shoulders with senior-level executives in a relaxed setting. After a couple drinks and a few good laughs, you never know what tidbits they may offer to guide the next phase of your career.

We would normally "divide and conquer," taking different sides of the room so that we could exchange notes from our respective watering holes. But eventually, we'd find ourselves in the same circle, surrounded by the sprinkling of other Black managers and directors. We considered these impromptu huddles sacred opportunities to let our guards down as Black people in predominantly white work environments. Almost intuitively, as other Black people see the gathering, they're drawn to it and upon entry crack a joke about "not getting the memo" that there was a meeting. It's the oldest joke in the book, but we erupt in laughter every time.

But one night, we watched one of our white co-workers bounce around from circle to circle, drunkenly meandering between groups. He made semi-coherent jokes but seemed to have no real target. Until he found one: our senior-level vice president—a married woman.

From a distance, we watched and hoped he would dig deep to collect himself, but instead he found the misguided courage to make a subtle yet obvious advance on her. We knew he was drunk and his reputation as a party boy preceded him, but we never thought he'd take it this far. In front of multiple direct reports and anyone else in full view from around the hotel bar, he inched his arm around her waist and began whispering in her ear until she gently and promptly dismissed him.

We couldn't believe what we had just seen, so we stepped in discreetly and escorted him to his room. But if you've ever tried to calm a drunk "frat bro" who just wants to have a good time, you can imagine what happened next.

First, he darted out of the hotel into the street and sprinted down the sidewalk. Concerned for his safety, we chased after him and were able to lure him back to the hotel and into his room. But he wasn't done. Minutes later, we saw him stumble out of his room and head back down to a different bar in the hotel. After trying to talk some sense into him, he finally agreed to call it a night but only after urinating on the lobby floor and issuing drunken, tearful apologies to everyone he saw along the way.

*This is not how we wanted to spend our night*, we both thought.

Our co-worker missed the closing breakfast plenary the next day. The following week, we saw him in the office and casually asked if he remembered any of what had happened that night. Of course, and perhaps conveniently, he didn't. Meanwhile, we were waiting for the ax to drop. We just knew that any day now he'd be called down to human resources to be informed his services were no longer needed, but it never happened. To our knowledge, he didn't even receive a warning.

A few months later, over lunch, he shared that a special role had been created for him, that he was promoted to director over a key project and was being groomed for an eventual VP position. Despite being less qualified than several other candidates and having a reputation for drinking one too many, he'd somehow managed to climb the corporate ladder in record time.

Was he good at his job? Sure. But he wasn't so talented to warrant immunity from consequences for unprofessional and, quite frankly, offensive behavior—especially not against a senior-level executive.

# The Fight Is Rigged,
# but There's a Way Out

We've heard too many stories of white co-workers who have somehow survived and grown in their careers after years of mediocre performance and continuous acts of reckless behavior. It's particularly gut-wrenching to hear our parents share versions of these stories because it illustrates how pervasive and long-standing this privilege is. Even for organizations and companies who commercially celebrate their diversity efforts, the proof—hiring—is rarely in the pudding. For Black employees, living through these experiences is like watching a fixed boxing match. As if the whole world watched someone get pummeled round after round but somehow repeatedly walks away with a win or, at worst, a draw from the judges' scorecard.

Extreme leniency can leave you feeling perplexed. But when you've seen privilege and bias play out over and over again in hiring and promotion decisions, the feeling quickly morphs from one of confusion to disillusionment, until it finally becomes affirmation. Instead of beating your head against the wall asking, how do I fix this, you begin to wonder, why even try?

The reason why it's important to try, despite everything stacked against you, is that all meaningful progress begins in your mind. We tend to talk about liberation movements and social change as if they just happen automatically, but they are the result of lots of individuals who took the first step and decided to change their own thinking.

First, you must tell yourself that you're not obligated to uphold the broken promises of an unfair labor model. Ask yourself questions that have the truth baked in. Like this one: If the fight you're in is rigged, what's the minimum number of rounds you need to hang in there before voluntarily throwing in the towel? Then, instead of doubling down on your career ambitions, ask yourself how quickly you can hop off the rickety ladder we've all climbed onto.

During our years of paying off more than $200,000 in debt, we had to dig deep to overcome the pressure we felt to uphold certain standards of living. Our ability to grow in our careers required us to dress in professional attire, maintain grooming and beauty standards, and network outside office hours. All of it cost money we could have invested or spent on improving our quality of life in other areas. But in time, we rejected the expectations—whether imposed by social systems or peer pressure—of co-workers, bosses, and, yes, even our loved ones, and cashed out for a life that was healthier and more aligned with our family's values.

It's very easy to become a victim of your circumstances, but if you can adopt an ownership mindset sooner—particularly one that's embodied in a set of practical tactics—you can interpret the things that are happening around you differently and use those thoughts to fuel your dreams of freedom. This starts with understanding that your true income-earning potential is far greater than any salary a company can offer you. To unlock this earning potential, you must invest your time and money in assets that have potential to appreciate in value. This could be real estate, intellectual property, licensing rights, stocks, or a business, to name a few. As you start to reap the benefits of ownership, such as property value appreciation, rent collected, tax benefits, portfolio growth, dividends, and profit, you'll be in the fortunate position of being able to compare income earned from those activities with the income earned from your job.

Having this perspective is truly transformative. And until you do, the idea of cashing out may feel like a pipe dream. But if you stay the course, over time you'll feel the shift in your mind and heart. You'll grow increasingly comfortable with risk and uncertainty. Most important, you'll find the courage to make decisions for your life that put your needs first.

## Expertise Is Not Required to Make Financial Progress

Look, we completely understand that managing money and redesigning your financial life are pretty scary. It's even more frightening when you're bombarded with a variety of conflicting information, too-good-to-be-true offers, and agents who pretend to have your interests in mind but really just want your money. But here's the good news. You don't have to be an expert to be financially successful or achieve financial independence. You don't have to achieve the same degree of mastery over personal finance that you have with your chosen field of work either. What you need is a fundamental understanding of how to make your money grow, the discipline to ignore distractions, and the courage to see it through.

When we started our blog in 2017, our writing had one

goal: to inspire better conversations about money. We weren't trying to persuade people to aimlessly walk away from their jobs or to choose specific investment options, because we understand those decisions are deeply personal and different for everyone. We'd meet people in person and online who loved what we were doing, and after striking up a conversation, we'd realize pretty quickly where they were on their emotional and financial journey. And in many cases, they were casual observers who hadn't taken the first meaningful steps toward preparing for their future. When we asked why, they would try to convince us they needed to read another book, check out another podcast episode, or take a course before getting started.

If you're one of those people, we understand your hesitancy. But the longer you delay taking action, the sooner you'll become prey to the network of gurus, marketers, salespeople, and platforms waiting on your inquiry. And the time and money you could be investing in yourself will be spent searching for all the answers to questions you may never actually encounter.

Let's say you're ready to invest and want more information about index funds. Like most people, you'd probably google "Are index funds a good investment?" On the first page of the search results, you'd see several recent articles. One might be called "Four Reasons Why Index Funds Are the Best Investment for Everyday Investors." Another, "Why the Index Fund Bubble Will Pop, Leaving Investors Out to Dry." You might even see conflicting articles on the same website, published days or even hours apart. Now you're doubting something you were pretty sure about a few minutes ago because there's clearly more to learn.

Confused yet? So, what do you do? (And what do most people do?)

Well, if you're frustrated, you may just go back to mindlessly scrolling through social media, telling yourself you'll figure it all out later. We get that. But if you're feeling frisky, you may walk further down the rabbit hole and click on one of the links. It may even take you to a website where you can open an account and buy your first shares of index funds, but the process will be confusing. There'll probably be language you've never heard of, and maybe the images on the first website are unappealing and bland. Because of this, you may convince yourself that *this company isn't the right one.* Assuming you haven't completely given up at this point, you may start to wonder, *Is there an easier, faster, safer way to do this? One of the social media personalities I follow keeps posting about financial stuff on Instagram; I wonder if she has a recommendation?*

None of this conflicting information or desire to seek help is by chance. It's actually intentional. According to a report by eMarketer, the financial services industry spent just under $20 billion in digital advertising in 2020, which is twice as much as in 2017. This doesn't include the books, courses, memberships, subscriptions, and funds spent by independent entrepreneurs and agencies all vying for your attention. If you're lucky, you'll escape this onslaught of conflicting messages without spending an unnecessary dime. But if you're like most Americans, you'll likely fall into a cycle of delay as you sort through all the junk or hand your hard-earned money over to a financial adviser who may not be legally obligated to act in your best interest.

As you start to apply what you learn, it's common to encounter roadblocks that may trigger you to want to learn more before taking additional steps. The key to overcoming these moments is recognizing that they're not always literacy issues. When financial illiteracy is viewed as the core problem, naturally financial education reveals itself as the only logical solution. And because so much of the financial media industry focuses on education to appease potential customers, many people get stuck on the learning merry-go-round without ever making any real progress.

You want certainty where certainty doesn't exist. You want guarantees that the financial decisions you make today will pay off in the future. Furthermore, you're underestimating the role learning in practice plays in your financial education journey.

Most savvy investors and successful entrepreneurs will tell you the hardest and most valuable part of their journey was overcoming self-doubt. The act of choosing to take that first step despite the discomfort, deciding not to sell when the market is down and to just keep going, is the most valuable part of the experience. So while you may believe education is the key to unlocking your wildest financial dreams, we're here to tell you it's only part of the solution. What you actually need is courage.

# Like It or Not, You May Never Feel Ready

The truth is that lots of millionaires are just people who had a moderate grip on the concepts we're covering in this book and were willing to try a few and see what worked. The people richer than you aren't necessarily smarter than you. They have simply taken more chances and survived more downturns than you have. They understand that in order to move past moments of uncertainty, they have to rely less on their cognitive abilities and tap into pockets of courage.

Think of wealth building as a kind of Fight Club. It's not a spectator sport; you have to be in it to truly get it. You don't learn how to fight by reading the autobiographies of the world's greatest fighters, do you? No, you learn how to fight by taking a few unwanted punches to the face and hopefully landing a few of your own. There comes a point where you have to be willing to press forward even though you have unanswered questions. You have to get out of your head and find the courage to *start*.

Finding the courage to act in the face of uncertainty is one of the most important aspects of cashing out.

## *The "Dwayne Johnson Effect"*

We all have narrow and specific images in our minds whenever we think about the word "courage." For instance, there's a good chance you're already conjuring images of the military, survivors of traumatic experiences, or people who have beaten enormous odds.

If we had to name a person who embodied the kind of courage we celebrate, it would be Dwayne "the Rock" Johnson. At six feet five, supremely talented with a jawline for days, the Rock is a celebrity, actor, producer, retired wrestler, former football player, and business owner with twenty-inch biceps. He is bravery personified and certainly America's preferred brand of confidence.

But it's all a sham. The Rock is just a persona built on top of a real human—Dwayne Johnson. As it turns out, Dwayne Johnson is deathly afraid of roller coasters. That's right. A man whose stage name literally means "a hard, large mass" is afraid of an amusement park attraction.

The fact that even our most profound image of confidence and courage is all a myth helps explain why none of us feel as if we can make a move in the midst of uncertainty. There is no way we can ever live up to this unrealistic, media-crafted image of courage, if even the Rock can't.

We call this paradox the Dwayne Johnson effect.

The truth is, we are all afraid of something. There is no such thing as full confidence. Instead, we must learn to move forward with a bit of courage.

One of the biggest problems with the myth of full confidence isn't that it exists; it's that it creates a culture where we insist on taking big risks just to prove that we are courageous. In other words, we become people who would rather swing big and miss than bunt every day and run the bases until they win. In part, this explains why millions of beginner investors threw caution to the wind in 2021, choosing to bet big on cryptocurrency and options trading, rather than less volatile and more proven approaches to investing.

The Dwayne Johnson effect also creates the impression that there's no need to tap into courage unless your back is against the wall or your life is hanging in the balance. In most cases it artificially inflates the stakes and makes them unnecessarily high. We convince ourselves that if we can quickly capitalize on these once-in-a-lifetime financial opportunities, we'll also be able to discreetly wipe away our past financial mishaps. In actuality, financial freedom is won more by the mindset shifts that we're discussing than by a lot of small, disciplined steps, which you certainly can take without understanding every aspect of wordy financial language.

## There's No Such Thing as Certainty

As comforting as it may feel to look for assurance in your investment outcomes, certainty doesn't exist in financial markets. And life still happens while you're busy investing.

Take popular retirement accounts like 401(k)s and IRAs (individual retirement accounts), for example. They're fantastic vehicles for stashing money, reducing taxable income, and growth. But when you invest in them, you're also betting that you won't need to touch that money until the later years of your life. If for any reason you need to access the funds in those accounts earlier than the qualified withdrawal dates, you'll be slapped with an early withdrawal fee (typically around 10 percent of the amount), and you'll have to pay income taxes on the amount you withdrew. In other words, you assume the best, but an unexpected life event during your working years can drastically throw off your retirement plans.

You can try to make the math work on paper or in your head, but when it's all said and done, whether your investment can cover your full retirement won't be a simple decision supported only by math. You'll need to grapple with an uncertain future where you may need to raise a child with special needs, care for an aging parent, or any number of special circumstances that you can't know in advance. In these cases, choosing to invest or not to doesn't make you reckless or brilliant; it makes you human. And sometimes, accepting your humanity irrespective of the outcome is the best thing you can do.

We learned this lesson the hard way once we became parents. We had read all the books, joined all the forums, and babysat all the kids in our family, but little prepared us for the day we brought our own child home and he was fully our responsibility. But we accepted that a human life was at stake, and despite not having the answers to all our questions, we agreed to take it one day at a time and figure it out. We trusted our instincts. And now, years down the line, we take tremendous pride in reassuring new parents that we didn't know how it was going to work out.

For those of us who have brains that like predictable outcomes, this idea that life is mostly unguessable can feel overwhelming. And there are a few thought patterns you should be aware of because if you can identify them every time they come up, you at least give yourself a chance to deal with them constructively, instead of letting them rule your subconscious.

The first is that when it comes to managing your money,

you need to avoid buying into the idea that if you don't feel 100 percent confident, it's because you don't know enough. If you can learn to use "I don't know" as an invitation to get curious, instead of a catalyst for fear, you'll make much more progress. When you find yourself saying you don't know, write down all the questions you have, and then cross out any of the ones that are looking for certainty where it doesn't exist.

Second, don't confuse uncertainty with risk. Uncertainty is an element of risk, but your uncertainty about something doesn't make it inherently risky. Think about it: you may be uncertain about how a date is going to turn out, but that doesn't make meeting up for coffee a risky exercise. When it comes to investing, the phrase "no risk, no reward" exists for a reason. Rather than avoid risks altogether, you need to find your sweet spot, or risk-tolerance level. Whenever you find yourself dismissing something because it seems too risky, take the time to get specific about which aspects of the opportunity are causing your red flags, and then ask yourself whether they can be managed or mitigated.

Going back to the index fund example, you need to get specific about why an investment feels like a risk. Is it the companies that make up the fund that are causing you grief? If so, you can look up their quarterly earnings or read commentary from financial analysts to help mitigate your concerns. Maybe it's market volatility that scares you. If that's the case, you can mitigate that by investing in more stable assets like bonds. Again, no amount of research will give you psychic powers, but it can help you move toward action.

# Small Acts Make a Big Impact

One of the questions we're asked most frequently is, "What is ONE thing you'd recommend people do if they want to live a rich and regular life?" We rarely answer it correctly because we don't want to feed into the notion that building wealth or becoming financially independent is as simple as doing one little thing.

Wealth building is a series of small acts of courage. There are no secrets, and there is no easy button hidden in our back pockets. Managing money, learning how to invest, getting out of debt, and tackling the interpersonal obstacles you experience along the way are hard work. We spent months oscillating on how to handle difficult conversations with our close friend and former financial adviser before finally opting to self-manage our retirement funds. We didn't want to make a mistake we would regret in the long run, and we didn't want to ruin a relationship that mattered to us. But we found the courage we needed to make the call, and today we have no regrets about the decision. Similarly, it took immense courage to tackle a conversation about debt early in our relationship. We knew the conversation had the potential to be explosive and it was, but we were able to piece things together, and our relationship grew stronger because of it.

You can read every bestselling book on the *New York Times* list, attend every seminar, subscribe to every podcast, pass every test measuring your financial literacy, and still find a reason not to take action. In those moments, the one thing we can offer you that best answers that question is to find the courage needed to do it anyway.

You don't have to reserve the courage you have deep within you for life-threatening moments. It's not a weapon only to be used in the event of unwanted intruders in your comfort zone. And it's not a bottle of wine that should be opened only on special occasions. Think of it as the fuel and oxygen you need to withstand the process of achieving your financial goals.

IN THE NEXT PART OF this book, "The Daily Struggle," we invite you inside our decades-long journey of uncovering the best methods of cashing out. We've curated the most effective list of financial advice, some of which comes from content we've consumed and used, as well as our own experience. We're offering you our best solutions, but you don't have to accept all of them to change something. You do, however, need a little courage to get started.

## rule

- **Paying yourself first is the ultimate act of courage.** You can choose to fully automate investing, semi-automate it, or do it manually, but it is critical that you do it FIRST. For beginners we recommend starting small and enrolling in one of the round-up programs from your bank or a brokerage. These programs operate off the purchases you're already making and round up to the nearest dollar. For example, if you buy a $2.80 coffee, the bank will round it up to $3.00 and the extra $0.20 would be diverted to saving or investing. From there, it's critical that you establish an emergency fund that contains several months of living expenses, then move on to create smaller stashes with sinking funds. A sinking fund is a strategic way to save up for things by putting a little bit of money away each month. It's a more specific way of giving your income a purpose, as we talked about in chapter 3. Let's say you decide to pay yourself $500 each month: you can create a few sinking funds and put $100 in index funds, $100 toward a future vacation, $100 for home renovations, $100 for an upgraded TV, $75 toward a new car, and $25 toward Beyoncé merch.

By the end of the year, you have thousands of dollars saved up. If something unexpected happens, you have a cash cushion that prevents you from tapping into your emergency fund. And on the flip side, when you decide to treat yo'self, you can use cash instead of a high-interest credit card.

## richual

- **Ask better questions.** If you've been reading carefully, then you've seen the role questions have played in our lives. Time and time again, our ability to ask better questions has saved us from ourselves. For example, asking "What is the purpose of income?" changed the way we thought about budgeting and allowed us to save more than any envelope system could have. Similarly, in chapter 7, we ask "How much are we willing to pay for an educated guess?" This question has saved us thousands of dollars in fees over a decade and will save us millions in our lifetime.

The act of self-auditing to determine when you're asking questions that are generative versus when you're just looking to be told what to do will lead you to the best version of yourself. This takes practice, but it's worth it.

# Part Two

# THE
# DAILY
# STRUGGLE

# CHAPTER 6

# Whatever You're Thinking, Think Bigger

One January morning in 2014, Jannese Torres-Rodriguez had a lightbulb moment. She was the only female engineer in her department and routinely felt underutilized, uninspired, and out of place. But considering she had $39,000 of student loan debt, $10,000 of credit card debt, and a $439,000 mortgage hanging over her head, she sucked it up—until she was suddenly laid off. Though the initial news came as a shock, she rebounded, choosing to see her predicament as an opportunity and not a death sentence. Having been inspired by FIRE podcasts and blogs, she'd already begun to explore the world of side hustling online and saw this as an opportunity to turn up the heat.

Jannese is passionate about cooking and noticed there was a gap in blogs that featured Puerto Rican and Latin cuisine. So after taking a food-blogging course, devouring YouTube videos, and learning about search engine optimization, she launched her first blog, *Delish D'Lites*. Two years later, she'd earned $2,295 and got her first taste of income earned without going into an office. It wasn't a life-changing amount of money, but it was a welcome trickle of cash flow in addition to the income from her new job.

Over the years, Jannese would continue to learn about affiliate marketing and apply the lessons to her blog and other side hustles. In 2020, she launched the *Yo Quiero Dinero* podcast, offered financial coaching and side-hustle coaching, launched an online course, and was a freelance writer, all in addition to her day job. And the results were nothing short of impressive. On top of the salary from her primary job, she earned an additional $100,000, which she used to pay off her student loans, crush her credit card debt, and boost her saving rate. By August 2021, she'd earned more than $200,000 online year to date and was smashing new revenue records every month. This additional influx of income led her to quit her job, putting her on track to be the first millionaire in her family and retire by the age of forty-five.

Was Jannese nervous about selling products and services online? Of course she was. "But I consider myself a mission-based entrepreneur. I know the value I'm putting out there on behalf of my business, and that makes it a lot less sleazy for me," she told us. "When life served me limes, I made *limonada*."

If the only way you create income is to exchange your time for money, you will inevitably run into three problems.

The first problem has to do with the agreed-upon rate assigned to your time—otherwise known as your hourly wage or annual salary. To raise this number, you need to be promoted, ask a manager for a raise, and likely make a strong case for why you deserve it. Even if you do all of that well, there's a long list of variables that impact whether you'll receive the raise you asked for, like budget limitations for your pay increase, buy-in from senior-level executives, and the reputation of the manager who is submitting the request on your behalf. This process can take months, sometimes years, and by the time you get the raise you feel you deserve, it may not be as financially impactful to you as it might have been in the beginning of the process.

Second, it's convenient to assume that all you need to do to earn more income from an hourly wage job is to work more hours. You might even be drawn to the idea of earning a higher hourly wage through working overtime or shift pay. But there are physical limitations to the total hours that can be worked. While "the grind" may be admirable and worthy of accolades by your peers on social media, it should be seen as a short-term and unsustainable solution to earning more money.

Work culture in America has made most workers one-trick ponies. Most of us only know how to exchange our time for money, and as a result we've become overly reliant on jobs as the single source of income and benefits to support our lives. This income myopia makes us vulnerable and can have devastating consequences.

The third problem is that many of the jobs we have come to rely on for income are slowly being eliminated as companies invest more in technology. In 2019, the former presidential candidate Andrew Yang became widely known for his campaign's signature program, "The Freedom Dividend." The premise of the program was to provide a universal basic income in the form of a $1,000 stipend for all Americans regardless of their work status. His justification for this proposal was simple. "As technology improves, workers will be able to stop doing the most dangerous, repetitive, and boring jobs. This should excite us, but if Americans have no source of income—no ability to pay for groceries, buy homes, save for education, or start families with confidence—then the future could be very dark," said Yang.[1]

The threat of technology and automation has particularly harmful effects on America's Black population. According to the 2019 McKinsey study "Automation and the Future of the African American Workforce," because so many of the jobs most at risk to automation are held by African Americans, the threat of job loss could compound poverty rates and worsen wealth creation for the Black community.[2]

For instance, "African Americans are overrepresented in the category of truck drivers, . . . [and] eventually, as much as 80 percent of a truck driver's work hours—the field's 'automation potential'—could be automated as technology rapidly evolves," the study says. The study goes on to offer suggestions on what could be done to reverse the pace of change and allow vulnerable communities to catch up.

But let's be realistic: What's the incentive for companies to slow down the pace of innovation? Why would we bet the security of our livelihood on institutions that have proven shareholders, not employees, are their top priorities? And who has time for any of these entities to figure it out? You need money now! So instead, you should be getting scrappy and creative to find ways to make money on your own. You should be leveraging these technological advancements and platforms to earn more money instead of burning more time.

## Technology: The Future of Wealth

If we had written this book in 2010, Kiersten would've been wearing crop tops and belly chains. Julien would've been obsessing over his first-generation iPad that he won at a raffle, even though he had no idea what real-world use it had. We also know that 80 percent of you would have been reading a paper version of this book because the Amazon Kindle was only three years old.

Now we can safely assume that some of you are still flipping pages, others are swiping or scrolling, and about one out of every five of you is listening to our voices as an audiobook. While print is still the dominant way people read, it's no longer the only way people read. As a matter of fact, in 2019 only 37 percent of adults admitted to reading only printed works.[3]

Advances in technology have changed the fabric of our lives, including how we earn income. Technology platforms have become cheap enough and user-friendly enough to be accessible to people who don't have a PhD in computer science. Consequently, we need to adapt new ways of earning money just as we've adapted to varying formats for consuming books. Making more money in the twenty-first century requires you to reconcile the role that technology plays in our culture, particularly online. Because of this, we believe technological literacy is just as important as financial literacy. And as I'm sure you can guess by now, Black and Brown communities are disadvantaged here too.

The digital divide has existed for a while, but a 2020 study from Deutsche Bank quantifies the impact as a function of time, not just skill level.[4] According to the report, Black and Hispanic communities have been ten years behind white communities for the last twenty years. During that time, the global digital economy has continued to grow exponentially. When you factor in the rapid automation of the U.S. economy, this divide could eventually mean the future Black and Hispanic workforce will be woefully unprepared for 86 percent of jobs in the United States by 2045.

If technological illiteracy threatens our future ability to gain meaningful employment in a digitized economy, the most crucial part of achieving financial freedom isn't in financial planning; it's in our ability to adapt to change. Historically, the American Dream has been inextricably linked to a linear pecking order. We're all socialized to just wait and hope we get picked. First you apply to a school and wait until they say yes; then you go to work and wait until somebody promotes you; then you want a house and wait until somebody gives you a loan; and so on. It's time to let go of that narrative. Tech entrepreneurs and digitally savvy people understand the moment we're in. They know the internet has made it easier than ever before to earn money, and they're taking full advantage of these advances in technology to build life-changing wealth every single day. Whether it's blockchain technology, crypto-currency, NFTs, or virtual reality, the tech savvy among us aren't waiting to explore the future of wealth, they're creating it.

## Ways to Make Your Own Money

Today, there are thousands of ways you can stop waiting on your boss to promote you and, instead, take the reins to your own life to earn money outside your normal 9-to-5. There are two factors you should be using to evaluate the options available to you: urgency and upside.

Whenever you're evaluating opportunities to earn more

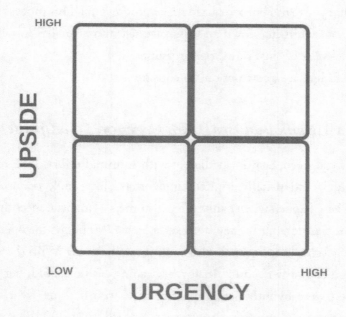

money, there's going to be a trade-off between the urgency of a situation (how soon you need the money) and the earning potential of an effort (how much money you could make). The goal of plotting opportunities this way is to take everything out of your head and condense your options to the ones most aligned with your immediate goal. In the words of Auntie Iyanla Vanzant, *you want to make the main thing the main thing.*

If you need money quickly, you'll want to focus on the opportunities on the right side of the matrix. If time is on your side and you can afford to explore slower opportunities, you'll want to focus on the left side. This way, you don't waste your time starting and stopping a bunch of too-little-too-late side hustles, and you don't create some ambitious financial plan that you're too burned out to make progress on. This process is about whittling down an expansive list into a smaller Goldilocks list of "just right" opportunities.

Here are a few options to consider.

## 1 | *Bank Bonuses (High Urgency, Low Upside)*

If you need cash immediately with minimal effort, look for quick and usually limited-time offers, like bank bonuses. These happen when banks offer customers a financial incentive for transferring money (for example, a $200 bonus for opening a checking account with a minimum balance). With these, you typically need to already have some cash on hand, but if you were hypothetically making three transfers per year, it becomes a low-effort way to earn upward of $1,000. Be sure to read the fine print, though, to ensure the reward will be deposited in your account within a reasonable amount of time. You can often find the latest great bank or credit card offers on popular websites like nerdwallet.com, thepointsguy .com, and bankbonus.com.

Other options in the high-urgency/low-upside camp are investment apps, which offer free stocks upon sign-up like public.com, acorns.com, and m1finance.com. Last, you may consider online survey companies like swagbucks.com that will pay out a small amount of money in exchange for your time.

## 2 | *The Gig Economy*
## *(Mid- to High Urgency, Low Upside)*

If you are willing to put forth slightly more effort than keystroking, you can explore the gig economy. The gig economy was born after the Great Recession of 2008 as a way to empower people who had extra time to earn money taking on small tasks, powered by technology. This gave rise to ridesharing companies like Uber and Lyft, grocery delivery companies like Instacart and Amazon Fresh, and handyman services such as taskrabbit.com. It ranks mid- to high from an urgency standpoint because once you sign up, the platforms do almost all the work to get you your first customers. It's also mid- to high on upside because with most of these platforms you don't have to sell a product; you just need to make yourself available and focus on providing good service.

But there are downsides. Income through gigs typically

doesn't come with benefits like health care or employer-sponsored investment plans. Many also have a reputation for being unsafe because you are engaging with strangers on a regular basis, entering their homes, or allowing them into your car. Last, as these companies grow and more workers sign up to earn more through the platforms, your earning potential can decrease due to a growing number of people making themselves available in your area. But assuming you are willing to take on these risks, have some free time, and are looking for a noncommittal way to earn extra money, jobs in the gig economy are one of your best bets.

In the past decade, the gig economy has expanded to include newer digital platforms that enable professionals to earn income based on their individual talents. One example is Fiverr, which is an online marketplace where skilled workers can exchange labor around the globe. Users can find everything from graphic designers, website developers, and writers to video editors within minutes and at a fraction of the cost compared with hiring a professional agency.

Joel Young is a pastor who used Fiverr to hire a voice actor for a small church project, and it sparked his own interest. At the time, he and his wife were knee-deep in student loan debt and brainstorming ways to pay it off quicker. He realized he already had all the equipment and decided to give voice acting a try himself. After eighteen months of selling voice-over services, Young made more than $1.5 million in income. When asked about the seven-figure benchmark, he told CNBC Make It, "To be honest, it's kind of snuck up on me."[5]

Joel's success is just one example of what's possible given

the size and the scale of the internet. Have you always wanted to be an interior designer? Great, there are platforms that connect you with people who want beautiful homes. Maybe you've always wanted to be a chef. Awesome! There are platforms that allow you to promote your culinary gifts and connect you with people who like to eat.

The same is true for writing. For example, Stacey Abrams is probably most famous for her work on voters' rights, but before she was a political force, she was a writer.[6] Yep, that's right, Stacey Abrams had a side hustle as the author of a series of steamy romance novels, which she published under the pen name Selena Montgomery.

New platforms designed to help you earn more are born almost every day, making it difficult to keep up with what's new. Thankfully, there are well-curated newsletters like *The Plug*, led by its founder, Sherrell Dorsey. In its own words, *The Plug* "shows the substantive ways that Black people are affected by and engaged with the innovation economy." It's available as both a free newsletter and a paid version to ensure you always have a steady pulse check on all things relevant in the fast-paced world of tech. You can also check out black freelance.com to guide you with the basics of getting started and finding a freelance community.

You should think of the gig economy the same way you would think of speed dating and test out a lot of different platforms to see which one suits you best. Whereas the first wave of service-based companies worked like a specialty store offering only one type of rigid work (for example, driving and delivery), the new platforms function more like an open market for you to sell your talents. If you can wrap your head around promoting your achievements on LinkedIn for prospective employers, then why not do the same in an open marketplace where employers, agencies, or other entrepreneurs can pay you for your talents without the long-term commitment. Whether you're a stay-at-home mom or someone with political ambitions, there is very little downside to generating extra cash online.

## 3 | *Arbitrage/Flipping Goods (Low Urgency, Mid- to High Upside)*

If you're willing to take on more effort for more upside, then get into "flipping," or the more technical term "arbitrage." Retail arbitrage is basically when you buy something cheap and sell it at a markup. Think of the people you see selling water on the sidewalk outside a stadium on a hot day. In a digital world, arbitrage could mean buying locally sourced goods on Craigslist and reselling them on eBay, or buying an existing product wholesale and selling it on Amazon. Arbitrage opportunities exist everywhere, in all asset classes. From hawking a pair of kicks or upselling baseball cards, to trading stocks or offering vacation rentals, you have many opportunities to make considerable profits.

The upside with arbitrage is its scalability. Unlike a gig opportunity, arbitrage can start as a side hustle and become something that generates full-time income without you needing to work around the clock. The biggest downside is the up-front cost. Not only are good deals hard to find, but you also bear the burden of the up-front investment without a guarantee of when or if it will sell. Depending on the category of products, it can take quite a bit of trial and error to become profitable, but once you get the hang of it, arbitrage is a powerful form of earning income passively.

Few people understand the intricacies of arbitrage like Jason Butler. Like many millennials, he graduated from college in 2008 and was thrust into one of the worst job markets he could imagine. But rather than throw in the towel, he stumbled into the world of arbitrage and has used it to supplement his income for the last decade. Over the years, he's tried almost every platform available before finding his niche with eBay. When he first started in 2016, he earned only $3,000 annually buying and reselling on the platform. As of 2021, he's on pace to earn an additional $14,000 between ebay.com, his preferred website, poshmark.com, and mercari.com. Jason's secret weapon is his passion for sports. He understands the genre so well that he specifically searches for memorabilia like bobblehead dolls, limited-edition T-shirts, or shoes and sells them at a markup to die-hard fans like him. Jason is such a side hustler that on occasion he's been known to drive to his favorite thrift store to pick up products, complete an Uber ride, and deliver for DoorDash on his way back home.

## 4 | *Digital Products and Courses (Low Urgency, High Upside)*

Digital products and courses have been all the rage in the early 2020s as people sought to both learn new skills and earn more money online. Not every course creator becomes wildly successful, but those who do usually go on to earn millions of dollars for selling a digital product they had to create, record, and upload onto a distribution platform only once. Instead of selling the course themselves to everyone they come across on the internet, they offer a commission to affiliates (for example, bloggers, podcasters, content creators, and other instructors) and in many cases students of the course to sell it on their behalf. So long as the commission paid out is built into the price of the product, everyone wins. Learners get access to information they need, affiliates earn a commission for a product they didn't create, and the owner earns a profit without lifting a finger. These are our favorite types of side hustles because they have unlimited upside and you have equity or ownership in something that grows without your daily labor.

If you've ever made and delivered a presentation to a group of people, either in person or online, then you likely have what it takes to create a digital product. As long as you have the ability to clearly communicate an idea and can attract a buyer, you can sell a digital product. The possibilities are endless, ranging from fifty-thousand-word ebooks or five-thousand-word e-guides, to ten-page checklists or a ten-module video recording. Pricing can vary widely as well. We've seen people sell PDF versions of a digital product for a dollar, ebooks for $10, or courses for upward of $5,000. Regardless of the path you choose, so long as the internet is working and your website is running, your product is available for sale while you spend your time focused on other things.

The process of creating digital products is straightforward. First, identify the problem you're solving for a prospective buyer. Second, create the product in a manner that best suits them. This could be an audio file, ebook, video, or even a series of emails delivered to buyers over time. Third, upload the product to an online platform. Last, promote the product to your buyers.

As of 2021, some of the best platforms for this include Skillshare, Amazon, Shopify, Teachable, Gumroad, and Kajabi. These platforms make the process of hosting, distributing, marketing, analyzing, and selling digital products easy because they provide all the key components of selling your product in one place.

## Me? Sell?!

Selling can be hard and feel unnatural. For many, it can even feel slimy, as if you were taking advantage of people. Selling also requires accepting a lot of rejection, which has the tendency to impact your self-esteem. But the internet is really big, and it takes only one yes to set a plan in motion. And thanks to faster internet connections, better cameras on phones, and mass adoption of e-commerce, your chances of getting that first yes are higher than they've ever been.

Now, even after providing several examples of other people who have successfully built new income streams, we typically receive pushback right around this point because of two things. The first is that the little voice in your head may be telling you, "I don't want to sell or promote my work online," "I'm too shy," or "I hate people."

This little voice may also be telling you that nobody wants to buy the thing you want to sell, or no one is willing to pay for what you have to offer. Well, allow us to remind you of an often-overlooked fact: you're already selling (and promoting) yourself.

If you work full time, you're already in the business of selling your time and expertise at a discount, given what we know about wage growth in the United States. The problem is you're selling to only one giant customer who could cancel the deal at any point and has a history of doing so. Between 1970 and 2002, the probability that a working-age American would unexpectedly lose at least half their family income doubled.[7] If you're reading this and are over fifty years old, chances are you'll be pushed out of your job before you're ready to quit.[8] So it might be a good idea for you to mitigate that risk the best way you can.

Continuing to believe wages or salaries from jobs are the only option for income is as extreme as continuing to believe that abstinence is the best option for sex education. It's a surefire way to reduce some harm, but is it sustainable? More important, is it fun?

One of the best books about sales we've ever read is *The Art of the Sale* by Philip Delves Broughton. The book features stories of some of the world's greatest salespeople, many of whom you've never heard of, like a Moroccan salesman named Majid. We love the way the author describes selling. He says it's "an endless confrontation with truth," and we couldn't agree more.

So, here's a truth: it's time to stop framing the options for your earning potential in stark terms around employment. We're not suggesting you do something erratic; we're asking that you put the "safety" of a W-2 income in its place. These days, earning additional income doesn't have to be as dramatic as quitting your job with no backup plan. Technology has unlocked the middle ground, and you can create an additional income stream in your spare time.

The tools to accelerate your income potential exist today. There's no gatekeeper, and you don't need permission; you need the same courage we talked about in chapter 5. At a time when the wage gap stubbornly persists and actually widens with career progression,[9] it's incumbent on us to decide that our worth is no longer a thing we have to prove to upper management over and over again. We can decide we're done waiting.

We've said it a few times already and now it's your turn. Say it out loud a few times: "I decide when I'm done waiting."

If this feels natural and permissive, then keep practicing it until it guides your actions.

But, if it feels awkward or goofy, pay attention to the moments when you're resisting. Write down all the places your mind says "yes, but . . ." because that's where you need to dig deeper.

It's time for you to accept that the internet is more than just a place for people to escape reality, stalk high school crushes, and share funny memes. It's also a global marketplace where billions of dollars in transactions are made every day. And the best part is, there are no barriers to entry, no qualifications needed or rounds of interviews required to get started. You need to believe you can do it on your own and be willing to overcome the fear of selling.

## ACHIEVE FI, FASTER

Establishing an income that is independent of an employer will not only give you a safety net but also accelerate your timeline to financial independence. We all know about the huge upside of compound interest, but one of the negatives is that unless you have a sizable amount invested, the growth is slow as hell in the beginning.

If you had $10,000 invested at a 7 percent return, in one year it would be worth $10,700. The next year, at the same return rate, you'd have $11,449. As long as your annual income is divvied out in small increments via a paycheck, it's going to take a long time for that 7 percent to get interesting.

Now ask yourself whether you think you could figure out a way to make $700 over the course of a year. If the answer is yes, then you should try. Because the beauty of compound interest is that the bigger the original balance, the more it compounds and grows. This is why that same $10,000 would be worth $20,000 in ten years, but then worth $40,000 in twenty. As long as you're dealing with small amounts, normal market returns are going to be slower.

# Content Creators Make How Much?!

In 2015, toward the latter part of our corporate career, one of the last projects we worked on was an influencer marketing campaign, which at the time was relatively new. In short, our company agreed to set aside budget to find influential people online who would be willing to post content about their experience with the company's brand. One guy was particularly intriguing because he was a Black father of two who celebrated the joys and pitfalls of parenting and wanted to break the persistent stereotype that Black men weren't active participants in raising their children. The other influencers were diverse couples and large families, all of whom had seemed to build out active audiences online who loved their content. These influencers seemed to be living the dream, and we often wondered, *Are they getting paid? And if so, how much?*

After doing some digging, we learned the Black father was paid $10,000 for his part in our company's marketing campaign. All he had to do was take two all-expenses-paid trips to our kid-friendly resorts, stay a few nights with his children, and eat at our restaurants. When he was done, we required that he post some pictures of his experience to his Instagram account, post a video to his YouTube channel, and write a blog post about his vacation linking back to our company's website.

Do you understand the words you just read/heard? A man who is not a celebrity by any means was paid $10,000 to take vacations with his family, take pictures, and write a blog post. And that's not all. When he was done, the company sent him some branded merchandise in the hopes he would post another picture with the children and their gifts.

Do you know what we would have had to do to earn a $10,000 raise at the same company?! We would have had to crush all of our intentionally lofty key performance objectives and gain the favor of peers both in and outside our core organization. We would've had to learn new skills and display measurable impact from those skills above and beyond our equally deserving peers in a single calendar year. We would've had to find an influential executive sponsor and serve as an admirable mentor to the younger workers below us. And we would've had to do it as Black professionals in a predominantly white work environment.

Even as real estate investors, at our peak our two properties delivered a consistent $1,300 a month. To earn another $10,000 in rental property income, we would've had to either find the cash-flowing deal of the century or pick up two more moderately profitable properties. This would've required us to save up a down payment for the loan, get insurance, conduct site visits, manage contractors, and hope an inspector doesn't find mold or termites.

The difference in effort required to earn $10,000 between this influencer and us was astonishing. Seeing this up close was the final push we needed to completely reevaluate not just how we viewed income as a whole but how we viewed income creation. It was clear, even back in 2015, that the future was digital. If we wanted to earn more, we needed to figure out a way to do it on the internet.

By 2019 and 2020, that's exactly what we'd done: we'd sold all our rental properties and channeled our efforts and resources into building more streams of income online.

To us, our blog was no longer just a place for us to share our intimate ramblings about money. It was digital real estate. It was also a distribution center where we could connect buyers and sellers of digital goods. It was a billboard where we could rent out space to brands for a temporary period of time for thousands of dollars. Most important, it was a place we owned where we could tell our story in our authentic voice, which attracted brands eager to access our readers and viewers. Instead of job hunting, asking for a promotion, or taking on more debt to acquire property, we dove into the world of digital entrepreneurship headfirst. We were starting to cash out.

> *Our blog was no longer just a place for us to share our intimate ramblings about money. It was digital real estate.*

In addition to our blog, we began earning money writing articles for websites. For the first article we wrote, we earned $250. A few years later, we were regularly invoicing brands and publishers for $750 to $1,250 for the same amount of work. We earned even more by monetizing our audience. In one case, we were approached by a brand to publish a post on our Instagram feed for $2,500. And the best part was they designed the post, wrote the caption, and provided the hashtags. All we had to do was hit the publish button at the agreed-upon time and send them a recap of how it performed.

In another case, we had an idea for a video we wanted to shoot for ourselves, but a brand representative reached out to us wanting to collaborate on a project, so we sold them the idea. Here's the kicker: we'd never shot or edited video before. But thanks to YouTube, in a week we figured it out. We gave them a pretty cool video they could use for twelve months, and we received $3,500 for a video shot completely from our iPhone in a few hours. So while the label "influencer" may make you think of self-obsessed millennials and Gen Zers who have nothing better to do with their time, you should know there are plenty of them who are earning significant amounts of money doing work they actually enjoy. The internet is a gold mine for making big money quickly with minimal effort. Unlocking its earning potential requires you to accept working in a faster-paced environment than you're likely used to and embracing innovation.

Since our introduction to influencer marketing, much has changed in the industry. Being an influencer is no longer considered a niche form of marketing as more mainstream brands are investing heavily in influencers as major parts of their brand strategy. The rise of the influencer has given birth to what is now called the creator economy, a more professional term that acknowledges how expansive the creators' marketplace has become and the value they provide to companies and customers.

If you're looking to explore this exciting world of content creators, here's how to get started.

First, identify the social media platforms you'll use as your primary means of building an audience. This should be solely based on where your target audience is, not necessarily what platform may be the largest, fastest growing, or most popular.

Next, build a brand or online personality that resonates with the audience you're trying to reach. Your objective here is to build genuine connections with like-minded people, so your logo, color choices, tone of voice, font style, and so on should be designed in a way that supports that purpose. If you're ever unsure of whether you've made the right design, it's best to ask others who may potentially be in your target audience for their feedback.

Last, communicate with your audience through those platforms and in a way that resonates with your audience consistently. This could be short-form video, long-form video, podcast, blog, livestreaming, in person, or simply via Twitter. The point is, your message should align with who your audience is, it should reside where your audience is, and it should be delivered in a way that meets your audience's preferences.

Becoming a content creator is a lot easier said than done, but when done well, and if recent trends continue, brands will be clamoring to collaborate with you. In essence, you'll become an intermediary standing between those brands and the people they want to be their customers.

## Letting Go of the Old Identity

Making the transition from corporate employee to digital entrepreneur requires you to dig deep. For us specifically, we had to overcome some emotional hurdles about income and identity. First, we needed to separate ourselves from the loyal corporate employees we once were. Admittedly, we'd lost sight of who we were without the company we worked for. Long after we left, remnants of our old jobs were still connected to so many parts of our life and home. The company logo was on our coffee cups, pens, beach towels, jump drives, bookbags, and even our son's clothing. So we purged it all to allow our old ambitions of climbing a corporate ladder and its corresponding identity to die peacefully. We were our own bosses now, and there were no ceilings to how much we could earn.

We've since learned that our sense of attachment to our careers wasn't unique to us. Both large and small companies spend a lot of money on fostering a culture that makes people feel as if they were part of a family. Because of this, when most people we know talk about their jobs or the company they work for, they tend to use pronouns like "my," "mine," and "we" as if they were the owners:

My company offers pretty good benefits.
We do things differently at XYZ corporation.
At our company, we get summer hours.

Employees regularly do this despite having minimal control over the company's direction and zero equity at stake.

The simple agreement of employment grows into a feeling of belonging until finally evolving into a sense of oneness. Your personal identity is devoured by your work identity, and in the process your potential is governed and dictated by managers. One of the best things you can do to avoid falling into this trap is to earn income on your own. Even if you don't go to the extent of creating a formal legal entity, the act of earning income that you've created or have full control over is one of the most empowering things you can ever do for yourself.

And that's perhaps the most rewarding part of making your own money, apart from wages or salary: When you cash out, you become *you* again. You reclaim your identity, and your work no longer defines who you are. That, to us, is freedom.

## rules

- **Your salary is not your ceiling.** The term "six-figure job" is often thrown around as a marker of success. The idea being, once you've reached this salary level, you've made it. But in reality, it means little, particularly if you're still underpaid for the value you provide. Instead of envisioning the six-figure salary as your ceiling, see it as a step on a staircase with infinite possibilities. Ensure that you're routinely investing in new skills and revisiting the value of your old ones by applying for new roles, or perhaps even freelancing.

- **Yesterday's price is not tomorrow's price.** One of the reasons people avoid taking action toward growing their income is because they don't factor in inflation. Inflation is usually described as a gradual increase in costs for discretionary goods like milk and gas. But it also applies to necessary goods like housing or services like health care. Because of this, over time, inflation diminishes your purchasing power, and since wages haven't come close to growing at the same pace, this should be a motivating factor to seek out additional income streams. Once you have an awareness of inflation, you can either adjust your spending, increase your income, or both.

## richual

- **Collect and measure qualitative inputs when assessing income-earning opportunities.** It's not enough to just measure income earned or the amount of work required between one activity and another. You should also track and compare how good it feels to earn it. A dollar earned doing something you enjoy is always better than a dollar earned doing something you don't. And if all else fails, just remember the phrase you've probably heard all your life, "all money ain't good money."

# CHAPTER 7

# Put Your Money to Work

One of the most important decisions you'll ever make as a young professional is how to invest your income. Because our respective stories on investing for the first time are so different, we've decided to tell them separately in our own distinctive voices.

## Financial Versus Fiduciary Adviser: Julien's Story

There are only a handful of moments in my life where I've come across new information and was so moved by it that I wanted to share it with the world. There was the time I heard *Midnight Marauders* by A Tribe Called Quest; this sent my love for hip-hop culture into overdrive. There was the day I learned I wasn't my father's only child and that I was actually the youngest of four. And then there was the day I learned the difference between a financial adviser and a fiduciary.

Throughout my twenties, I invested regularly in my 401(k).

It wasn't much and I didn't really understand what it was, but whenever I had questions, I could always rely on Martin. He was a family friend and my mother's financial adviser. He worked for a reputable financial services company, lived in a nice house, and was the model for what I would consider a successful Black man. I'd been to his wedding, dined in his home, and took counsel from him far above and beyond managing my financial future. For all intents and purposes, he was a mentor and still is to this day.

As my financial adviser, Martin's job was to take the money I gave him and make it grow. And he was honest, forthright, patient, and incredibly thoughtful when doing it. There were times he advised less aggressive investments after learning about my recent life changes. And when I gained confidence in my career trajectory, he'd step in and advise me to play a little more aggressively. His thought process was simple: if I didn't need the money today and had no use for it in the near future, it was probably a good idea to put it in the market. From my vantage point, he was damn good at his job, and I happily recommended him to anyone who was looking for a financial adviser. But as I began to develop my own point of view on investing, it forced me to reconsider the nature of our relationship.

Like most people I know, I didn't believe I could manage my retirement planning by myself. Instead, I was much more comfortable handing that part of my brain over to a professional. Like doctors and lawyers, I believed, they had credentials and the ability to analyze information in ways I would never have. The difference between doctors or lawyers and a financial adviser, however, was that I was a bit clearer on how they were compensated. I knew that if I needed a medical procedure done, the hospital or doctor's office billed my insurance company, and so long as I paid my premium, the services were covered. Similarly, if I found myself in hot water and needed a lawyer, I could hire one who billed me by the hour.

I could also assess the value of what I paid for. Was I still sick or in pain? If the answer was no, then it was fair to say the doctor did his job. Did I spend the night in a cold dark cell wearing an orange jumpsuit? If the answer was no, then the lawyer did a good job and I got my money's worth. But I couldn't say the same for Martin, because I had no clue how he was compensated. All I knew was I never received a bill and there were no line items for advisory services on my statements. It all seemed very opaque, and over time I admittedly grew suspicious.

One day, after years of working and investing with him, I couldn't help but feel bothered by the minimal growth in my account. To be fair, I wasn't making contributions regularly, but when I'd watch the news, it was clear to me the stock market was booming, which led me to wonder, *Shouldn't my balance be growing?*

It was the early 2010s, the market had crawled out of a huge slowdown, and almost everything was looking up. Everything except my IRA, that is. *Did we bet on the wrong stocks? Should we sell that weird 2050 Transcontinental Long-Term Growth thingamajig and buy more Home Depot?* I saw plenty of homes being built, and their parking lot was always full. Surely business was good for them. What was I missing?

I decided to do research on my own so that I was better prepared for the next time we spoke. At this stage in my life, I didn't want to continue nodding my head in approval like some bobblehead doll every time Martin made a recommendation. No, I wanted to understand what he meant, what I was invested in, and why. And after reading books and blogs and watching documentaries on the subject, I was shocked by what I learned.

First, the information I consumed demystified how financial institutions and advisers were paid and seemed to explain why I wasn't seeing the kinds of increases I'd hoped for in my IRA. Second, these new insights all led me to the same solution—index funds. Investing in index funds had been around for decades but had been cast as a boring, predictable, and lazy approach to investing. Nevertheless, I was intrigued and ready to give it a try.

There was only one problem. When I told Martin what I'd learned and that I was interested in investing in index funds, he seemed a little hesitant. This was because, in order for him to do what I was asking him to do, he'd have to sell the stocks and mutual funds I'd already invested in and re-allocate the funds into index funds. Well, the company he worked for didn't offer those funds or anything remotely like them. And the reason they didn't offer them was that index funds didn't make them any money.

It turned out Martin's pay was largely based on commission. Whenever any of his clients purchased specific funds or financial products he recommended, he earned money from that transaction. As my financial adviser, while it was his job to grow my portfolio, he also had a vested interest in doing it in very specific ways. Even more shocking, he was not legally obligated to make recommendations that were in my best interest. In theory, he could recommend funds that earned him and his company a handsome commission, even if they were not the most cost-effective for me. In legal terms, Martin was a *financial* adviser, not a *fiduciary* adviser.

Financial advisers provide financial services such as managing your investments, choosing an investment strategy, and helping you adjust your approach as your life or goals evolve. In short, they help people make sense of the complex financial world by shaping their decisions.

Fiduciaries, by definition and law, follow what is known as the fiduciary standard: a set of legal principles established by the U.S. Securities and Exchange Commission or state regulators. They are legally bound to follow standards that ensure they put their clients' needs first. Martin was not bound to follow this code at all. That's not to suggest he didn't have or follow a code of ethics; he most certainly did. But there was a direct conflict of interest between what shaped his recommendations and what shaped my new, more well-informed investment goals.

Learning this explained his hesitation when I made the initial request to take a different approach with my portfolio.

Normally, he was responsive, quick to invite me to his office or arrange a call to talk more about my financial future. But when I recommended taking a course of action that didn't align with his company's interests, he froze, and weeks went by before we could actually talk about it. It was unlike him, and I'd started to wonder if maybe I'd struck a nerve. When we finally connected, he admitted that he understood my perspective and felt the rub between doing what I was asking him to do because it conflicted with what he was assigned to do for his job. Our client relationship ended shortly after that, but luckily we were able to retain a friendship—one that didn't have any misaligned objectives or hidden terms and conditions.

This experience was eye-opening for me because it revealed just how many people I knew had completely given away the direction, trajectory, and growth potential of their life savings to people who aren't required to make decisions in their best interest. It partially explained why so many people I knew were so flippant about investing: many of them felt they were already doing the right thing by having a financial adviser. To me, it was one of the earliest indicators of how powerful marketing had become and how it shaped the way most people thought about their money.

## The Power of Index Funds: Kiersten's Story

I began my investing journey with a retirement fund. At my job, I was eligible to participate in the 401(k) program after ninety days, but I ignored it for five years because the horror stories from the 2008 Great Recession were enough to dissuade me. Besides, I liked my money where I could spend it, and the thought of making my paycheck even smaller was out of the question. I had a narrative running in my head that making money was easier than managing it, so I spent my twenties focusing on climbing the corporate ladder and believed I could save whenever I was ready.

Like most of my peers, I was smart enough to understand that the value of an investment was supposed to increase over time, but I was still thinking about it in a linear way. I was using the terms "saving" and "investing" interchangeably and completely underestimated the exponential role that compound interest played. In my mind, if someone had a million-dollar portfolio, they had worked for and saved most of those dollars. So naturally, I told myself that I needed to make way, way, way more money before I could even *think* about investing.

Turns out I was wrong.

After some candid conversations with mentors where they showed me the cost of my avoidance, I finally took the first steps to preparing for my future. I immersed myself in the financial education world to see what I was missing. You've heard of a die-hard student? Well, I was a try-hard student. I really wanted to understand everything, all at once. I dove headfirst into the personal finance world and was being nagged by everybody from Suze Orman to Dave Ramsey to David Bach. I was still haunted by my past choices and internalized their opinions with the hopes of drowning out my own. It didn't take much time before I could recite their advice better than they could. I was doing all the right things—denying myself the things I wanted, snowballing my debt, and making lattes at home—but I still didn't have any investments.

So, I decided to take a look at my employer-sponsored 401(k). At that time, the company offered a 100 percent match on up to 6 percent of my salary, and I hadn't taken advantage of it for five years. I was embarrassed about how much free money I had left on the table and that was enough to motivate me to take immediate action. Even though I was terrified of messing up again, I mustered up the courage to log on to my computer and finally enroll in my 401(k) plan.

The bright screens and interactive tools welcomed me just as my grandma does when she hasn't seen me in a while. The interface wanted to know more about me and my "investing style," whatever that meant. It asked me about my financial goals, and my type A heart fluttered as I glided my mouse arrow across sliders built into calculators that spit out really sexy numbers. Everything was customized and colorized in a way that made me feel confident and in control. It was simple to select whatever they told me I wanted. And did I mention there were worksheets? There were worksheets! I love worksheets!

Throughout the process, there were friendly prompts asking me questions. *Do you want to take advantage of "catch up" contributions?* Sure! How'd they know? *Do you want to go with these preselected options?* Why not! *How much money do you think you'll need in retirement?* Ummm . . . a lot! Let's go with an aggressive stock mix! Hell yeah. I checked boxes with glee, grinning like a bride with no budget. It was like shopping for a future life!

My imagination went wild as I played with the calculators to figure out how much I'd need to set aside if I wanted to have a yacht waiting for me in my golden years. And before I knew it, I was enrolled. I had no idea what I had clicked on, but after years of no activity I felt good about the life I was creating for the future me. In that moment, getting it done was more important than getting it right.

A few months later, I learned about index funds. They made so much sense that I thought, that *must* be what I signed up for. When I went back to the 401(k) portal to confirm, I realized I was enrolled in funds that were almost ten times more expensive than the index funds that were offered. If I'd continued to invest that way, it would've been almost impossible to live the life I'd imagined, because the fees on those funds would eat up my returns. I had naively assumed the bank and I had aligned interests. While I had done well by investing, I had also clicked, selected, and responded to on-line prompts assuming it was all solid financial advice. Really, it was all marketing to make *them* money on fees.

So, I changed my portfolio mix to invest predominantly in index funds. It was scary, but for the first time in my adult financial life I felt confident and in control. And I haven't looked back since.

I had spent the majority of my professional career working in business development and marketing organizations, so if there was one thing I knew how to do, it was to communicate an idea to someone in a way that moved them to act. Yet it never occurred to me that while I was making investing decisions with my employer-sponsored 401(k) plan, I was the one being marketed to. The postcards in the mail, app notifications, happy birthday emails, and fancy free calculators in my dashboard—they were all designed to get me to give them more of my income. And because I'd assigned so much virtue to investing, I assumed the details were irrelevant and just believed that whatever they offered would be good for me. My blind optimism could've cost me my retirement, but it was a turning point as an investor and the beginning of my journey to redefine what it means to be empowered.

## How Much Are You Willing to Pay for an Educated Guess?

Index funds should be a core component of your investment strategy because they ensure you have some skin in the game of this great American experiment. Throughout history, the United States has seen its fair share of peaks and valleys, from wars on its own land and conflicts abroad, to natural disasters and struggles for equal rights. We could go on and on about the number of times we, as a country, have been pushed to the brink.

But through it all, our leaders, elected officials, and institutions have remained steadfast in their protection of our financial markets. This is because they know how critical they are to the overall health of our country. Whether you agree with this degree of prioritization or not, the fact remains the stock market is a treasured part of American society and in many ways the heart of American life. And owning index funds is like owning a tiny slice of America.

As a working citizen, you owe it to yourself to stake your claim. You owe it to your family to ensure they have their fair share of the harvest. And you owe it to those who came before you to make the most of the access and power you've been granted.

It's not unusual to meet people who have never heard of index funds, especially if their primary investment vehicle has been an employer-sponsored retirement plan like a 401(k) or 403(b). And to understand why we love index funds so much, you need to first understand how they differ from their sound-alike, mutual funds.

## *Mutual Funds*

Mutual funds are a specific selection of stocks and/or bonds that are grouped together and sold to investors. The reason they're grouped together is to give investors a wider degree of exposure by owning a bunch of stocks or bonds instead of individual stocks or bonds. That way, if a few of your investments don't do well, you aren't at risk of losing all your money. Most mutual funds are also designed to beat the market, which means that however the market is performing, mutual funds are aiming to do better. If analysts are predicting the market will increase by 7 percent, these funds are shooting for 8 percent,

9 percent, or more. This process of combining, analyzing, predicting, rebalancing, and attempting to exceed the stock market's expected growth is called active management. So who does all of this work? Who determines what goes into an actively managed fund?

Stock pickers, fund managers, and analysts make daily, sometimes hourly decisions to choose the collection of mutual fund holdings. They use data, technology, and sophisticated modeling to make educated guesses about which selection of which funds is likely to outperform the stock market as a whole. Think of these financial professionals as you do your favorite sports analysts on ESPN. These men and women eat, drink, and sleep sports. They can put last night's game into historical context and make bold predictions about who's going to bring home the big trophy, and they all have opinions on who will be the year's Most Valuable Player. Fund managers basically do the same thing, except they analyze stock markets and wear less colorful outfits.

When a financial analyst is done picking all of their hot stocks and bonds, they package them into a mutual fund. These funds are then sold (yes, sold) to you by someone like Martin, or they're sold to your retirement plan sponsor (employer), who then lists them as investment options for you to buy with your retirement contributions.

In the end, the fancy financial analysts, managers, and advisers are simply making educated guesses.

Now, here's the kicker: you have to pay for this educated guess whether it's right or wrong. And that's what makes index funds so much more attractive.

## Index Funds

Index funds are a type of mutual fund except for one key difference: they are passively managed. In other words, there aren't nearly as many geeks in some back room looking at screens making guesses about which stocks will outperform others. Instead, when you buy an index fund, you're buying a whole market, category, or sector of funds. For instance, if you purchase an S&P 500 index fund, you are essentially buying a piece of *every* stock listed on the S&P 500. Similarly, when you purchase a Nasdaq index fund, you're buying a piece of the entire Nasdaq as a whole. The goal here is to minimize the risk of losing money due to the poor performance of any particular stock and to invest in the market, category, or sector as a whole. And, because index funds don't require nearly as much elaborate, constant analysis and hand selecting, they typically cost a fraction of what an actively managed mutual fund does.

Let's change gears for a second and go back to sports. At any given moment, if you turn on ESPN, you'll see a collection of analysts, reporters, and former players rambling about which team is in the best position to win a championship in any given sport. They'll talk about the roster, coaching, lingering health issues, home-team advantage, and even immeasurable metrics like tenacity, teamwork, and the will to win. Even with droves of data and their respective "feel for the game," each of these analysts is merely offering an informed and sometimes entertaining opinion.

Now, you could bet on *one* of these analysts, say Charles

Barkley, guessing correctly. That would be like investing in a mutual fund. Or, instead, you could bet on the fact that sports fans will continue to watch sports. Doesn't the latter feel like a more certain bet?

Let's use the National Basketball Association as a specific example. One day, LeBron James is noted as the greatest basketball player we've ever seen. The next, Kevin Durant is given the crown after a stellar playoff performance and winning a few championships. Then, seemingly out of nowhere, a player from Greece, Giannis Antetokounmpo, and another from Slovenia, Luka Dončić, are breaking records and poised to be the true stars of the league. If you're a fan of the game, this is perfectly fine and maybe even fun to keep up with the ebbs and flows of the NBA spotlight. But this is no way to manage your retirement funds, especially if you're paying a premium for an educated guess. It's far safer to bet on the fact that millions of fans around the world will continue to tune in to watch these amazing athletes compete for the foreseeable future.

When you're investing in index funds, you're betting on the fact that overall a given index will continue to deliver favorable results. You understand that some companies will succeed and fail far beyond anyone's imagination, but you don't let those individual wins or losses distract you from the overall performance of the market. This is because you're paying attention to the market as a whole and its performance over the long run, not day to day.

If this sounds boring to you, then congratulations . . . you get it! But don't assume this approach doesn't pay off. On average, the U.S. stock market has historically produced a 10 percent annualized average return. When adjusted for inflation, that return is about 7 percent. But that 7 percent return will have a huge impact on a portfolio over time. A $500 monthly investment growing at 7 percent blossoms to more than $155,000 after fifteen years. After twenty years that same investment grows to just under $254,000, and after thirty years it balloons into $584,000. This is the power of simply investing in an index fund instead of paying a premium by trying to beat it.

There are hundreds of indexes set up to monitor the performance of various markets, sectors, and investment strategies. Likewise, there are index funds that track five hundred of the largest companies in the United States like the S&P 500, or a group of smaller, promising companies. There is little if any intense analysis needed here because, again, the objective of these funds isn't to beat the market; it's just trying to follow the crowd. So if the Dow or the S&P 500 is up, then the market is considered to be doing well. Conversely, when these indexes are down, you can think of the market as doing poorly. Your index funds will do the same, but over time, on average, you will have significantly more good days than bad.

Widely known as one of the world's wealthiest people and savviest investors, Warren Buffett once wrote in his annual shareholder letter, "My regular recommendation has been a low-cost S&P 500 index fund."

## Taxes and Fees

Whenever you buy a mutual fund, whether it's actively or passively managed, there are fees associated with owning it as well as ongoing operating costs like advisory fees related to managing the fund's holdings for your adviser, marketing, and legal. These fees are called the expense ratio and are expressed as a percentage of your investments, such as 0.2 percent or 3.0 percent. Understanding how they're calculated can be a little tricky; nevertheless, comparing the cost of mutual funds should be top of mind when choosing to invest.

Here's an example of how this works. (Note: we've rounded some of these numbers to make them easier to understand.) Let's say you invested $10,000 in a mutual fund within your tax-advantaged retirement account with a 1 percent expense ratio and allowed that money to compound over forty years. Assuming the market grew at an annual rate of 7 percent, with no other contributions that $10,000 investment would result in a gross value of just under $150,000. That's the magic of compound interest, but that's not the number you as an investor would have in your account.

Because the fund charges a 1 percent expense ratio on the total value of the holding, you'd actually have $102,000 with $48,000 going to fees. That presumably tiny 1 percent fee would erode 32 percent of the total value of your investment!

Now let's say your slightly more intelligent (and, dang it, also more attractive) twin made a $10,000 investment in an index fund on the same day you did, also made no further contributions, and allowed it to grow for the same forty-year period. The only difference is the expense ratio on their fund was 0.04 percent instead of the 1.0 percent you paid. At the end of the forty-year period, your evil twin would have $148,000 in their account, having paid a little over $2,000 in fees. The

0.04 percent fee they paid would account for only 1.5 percent of the fund's total value.

But wait, there's more.

As proud citizens of the United States, you both need to pay taxes on your income. So, if you both decided to withdraw the entire amount after the forty-year period to spend on your celebratory retirement trip around the world, you'd both need to pay taxes on your withdrawal. Assuming you're also both average Americans who pay the typical effective tax rate of 13.5 percent,[1] you can expect to deduct another chunk from your respective balances, leaving you with $88,230 while your sexy, evil, and now richer twin would have $128,020.

While this is a hypothetical situation, does it feel good knowing that after a lifetime of working hard and investing, in your golden years you can only really rely on being able to live off a little more than half of what you should have earned with your $10,000 retirement investment? About one-third of your investments went to the financial services company that managed your money and another portion of what was left went to the U.S. government. In that scenario, you'd have spent the first eighteen years of your life unable to work, the next forty-seven years of your life working, and the remaining time you had left nibbling on half of the pie you spent a lifetime baking. That is the unfortunate reality of most aspiring retirees.

According to a 2014 study by the Center for American Progress, "On average, American workers' 401(k) plans charge fees of approximately 1 percent of assets managed." To make matters worse, almost eight out of every ten (77.97 percent) actively managed mutual funds in the United States under-performed the S&P 500 as of June 2020.[2] So not only are most mutual funds way more expensive than index funds, most of them have a history of underperforming the market. Fund managers are charging you to lose your money! Yet this is the reality of most American retirees. It turns out the only thing hypothetical about this situation for the average American worker is having an evil twin sibling they don't know about.

## The First $100,000 Is the Hardest (Here's How We Did It!)

Immediately after we broke up with our financial advisers and decided to venture into the world of self-managing our investments, it's safe to describe our general mood as cautiously optimistic. After all, we were venturing into a world of investing for the very first time armed with nothing more than our own understanding of what to do next. There was no Martin to send an email to or jump on a call with to help validate our decisions. But there were also fewer hands in our pockets shaving off our returns and leaving us with whatever was left after their fees had been taken out.

Some days it felt as if we were drinking from a water hose, but over time we adjusted to this new level of responsibility. At this point in our relationship, we'd moved in together and were also starting to merge our lives and finances. This required us to have regular conversations to review our budget, portfolio growth, and financial goals. It also required us to be transparent about our spending and mutual acceptance of risk. It took us a few months, but we eventually found a rhythm and approach that worked for us.

We received paper checks from our advisers after closing our accounts and forwarded them to Vanguard, our investment firm of choice. Its founder, the late Jack Bogle, is widely regarded as the father of indexing, having championed the investment approach for years. Furthermore, the firm was often quoted as the gold standard in the FIRE community for its service and affordability, so we felt comfortable in our decision to invest with it. Over time, we would park some of our earnings in other investment houses like Fidelity, Ally Bank, and Betterment. All of them offered index funds in some shape or form, and we wanted to make sure we had something to compare our original decisions with.

After paying termination fees from our former investment firm, what remained was around $10,000 total, a nice round number that allowed us to easily calculate growth in our heads month over month. While we don't obsess over our portfolio daily anymore, we were mindful of it at the time, given the decision we'd made to cut ties with our advisers. A month after our first investment in Vanguard's flagship Total Stock Market Index Fund, our statement had already shown an increase of approximately $700, and we were over the moon. For years we'd grown accustomed to flat if not minimal growth every month, and while we knew our balance could quickly slide in the opposite direction, we were simply happy to see signs of life.

We'd also gone into our respective employer-sponsored

401(k) plans and completely reallocated our portfolio. We said goodbye to the guessing game of parking 35 percent here, 20 percent there, 15 percent international, and the rest in some confusing fund we knew nothing about. Instead, we kept it simple, though aggressive, by allocating 90 percent of funds in an institutional version of Vanguard's Total Stock Market Index Fund and the remaining 10 percent in a bond index fund to offer a little bit of stabilization to our portfolio.

Having committed to living on significantly less than we earned, we both decided to max out our respective 401(k)s and did that consistently for the remainder of our professional careers. On occasion, whenever we received a surprise influx of cash, we'd invest in a separate taxable brokerage account purchasing, you guessed it, more index funds. Across all our accounts, there were several days between 2016 and 2018 where we'd see dramatic $10,000 changes to our net worth in a single day. To be fair, there were periods where we'd see $30,000 declines in a monthly statement. But overall, like the climate in the Caribbean, the good days significantly outweighed the bad.

Even as entrepreneurs, we've continued to invest consistently in index funds. As a result, our three accounts in addition to HSAs and 529 plans have grown handsomely. Assuming we don't touch that money and make no further contributions and the market performs at its historical average of 7 percent, compounded annually, that portfolio will grow to upward of $4 million dollars over the next twenty-five years. That's a big chunk of pie!

This, in addition to the market value of our home, the growth of our business endeavors, intellectual property, and other assets we own, has given us a deep sense of peace and courage to live a life aligned with our values. In short, we work because we choose to, not because we have to.

## "Why Would I Do That?"

There's an old saying that goes a little something like this: "When you know better, you do better."

We don't believe that for one second.

If that were the case, we'd all do a much better job of eating vegetables, drinking water, and respecting each other as human beings, wouldn't we? In the real world, the act of knowing better gets you only halfway there. The other half is navigating life and juggling priorities while trying to keep your shit together. So now that you know index funds are powerful, reliable, and affordable investment options, let's start building a protective shield around this newly formed point of view so you aren't deterred by the onslaught of distractions wedged in between you knowing better and you actually doing better.

Right now, we want you to say these five words out loud: "Why would I do that?" This simple phrase is precisely what we want you to say to yourself or to anyone else who may be offering you a complicated or costly alternative beyond the simplicity of index fund investing. We can give you the clarity and confidence you need to start investing wisely, but only you can give yourself the courage to stand firm in your decision and to walk away from the distractions that are sure to come.

If a friend sends you an invitation to meet up for drinks and casually suggests starting an investment club because there's a lot of money to be made investing in hot stocks, we want you to say, "Why would I do that?" You now know that for average investors stock picking is a fool's game and it's much wiser to invest in a wide selection of funds than relying on faulty intel to hand select a few.

When a family member corners you at a BBQ, starts showing you receipts from their latest multilevel-marketing business, and invites you to the business opportunity of a lifetime, we want you to say, "Why would I do that?" You now know that you can take that same entry-level fee they're asking you to pay and use it to invest in an index fund where it is much more likely to produce a positive return without your lifting a finger or potentially dragging someone else into the fold.

Deflecting against these distractions is critical because in all our years of speaking with people and couples about their finances, we've found that the main reason people lose out on opportunities to make their financial lives better is pressure from outsiders or the fear of conflict. Like you, we were not exempt from these feelings. In the beginning of this chapter, Julien shared his own experience with a financial adviser. Because that adviser was also a family friend, choosing to go in another direction was incredibly difficult and added weeks to the decision-making process.

For you, your adviser may be an actual family member, someone who attends your church, or a key figure in a professional organization you've joined. All of these close ties make it even more challenging because you don't want to suggest the person is taking advantage of you or may not be an expert in their field. That feeling has a name—insinuation anxiety. A 2019 Carnegie Mellon University study defines insinuation anxiety as "concern that rejection of advice may be interpreted by an adviser as an indication of distrust—a signal that the advisee may view the adviser as biased or corrupt."[3] By asking them, "Why would I do that?" it may put them on their heels a little, but it also forces them to defend their recommendations.

Now that you have a newly sharpened point of view, the conversation is much more objective, not personal. Your friends and family are entitled to have a preference for actively managed funds, and you're entitled to prefer a simpler, stabler, and more cost-effective approach. They're allowed to charge high fees for the work they do, and you're allowed to politely decline their services. They're permitted to make recommendations that earn them a considerable commission, and you're permitted to put your family's future first.

BEING ARMED WITH the true cost of investing and the power of low-cost index funds is like being officially knighted into a growing invisible army of savvy, like-minded investors around the world. You have your clear marching orders and a shiny new protective shield to prevent the enemy from infiltrating your pockets. But it wouldn't hurt to have some encouraging words taped to the inside of your shield to help keep you focused in the event of a surprise attack. Here are some rules on investing to help you along the way.

# rules

- **Fees are a four-letter f-word.** The magic of compounding interest works in both directions. It can be either a mighty force that pushes you forward or a parachute on your back making it all but impossible to sprint. It's easy to see a single-digit percentage, and assume it's a minuscule amount. But in reality, we should think of it this way:

  For a $10,000 investment, over forty years, assuming a standard 7 percent rate of return, a:

  - 1.0 percent fee equals one-third of the total value (expensive)
  - 2.0 percent fee equals just over half of the total value (ridiculously expensive)
  - 0.5 percent fee equals about 17 percent of the total value (affordable)
  - 0.1 percent fee equals about 4 percent of the total value (ideal)

- **Your money can work harder than you can.** We've all been taught the value of an education and the importance of a strong work ethic. The combination of both and following a strong moral code are supposedly the core ingredients for a good and successful life. Unfortunately, the data suggests, it's simply not enough. According to a 2018 Pew Research Center study, "After adjusting for inflation, . . . today's average hourly wage has just about the same purchasing power it did in 1978, following a long slide in the 1980s and early 1990s and bumpy, inconsistent growth since then."[4] This means that despite advances in productivity, the average American is only slightly better off than they were almost forty years ago.

Conversely, over that same period of time, between 1980 and 2020, a $10,000 investment in a simple S&P 500 index fund would have grown into almost three-quarters of a million dollars requiring no work at all. So, while it's admirable and virtuous to pride ourselves on our abilities to work hard, the potential value of our labor is unfulfilled when income isn't converted to investments. It's fine to work for money, but it's far better to have your money work for you. You can find a full list of our favorite investing tools and apps on our website at richandregular.com/resources.

- **Don't believe the hype.** There have been a handful of notable stock market crashes (bear markets) in modern history. There's the 1929 Great Depression, the 1987 crash known as Black Monday, the bursting of the dot-com bubble in 2000, and the financial crisis of 2008. After each of these crashes, the financial media pounces on the story, stoking fear and whipping the general public into a frenzy with concerns about our country or global markets falling apart.

Then, without fail, things start to bounce back, and the financial media celebrates the remarkable achievements of the public and private sectors for bringing us all back to the prosperity we've come to know and love. All is fine in the world and we can get back to expensive vacations, luxury cars, and fancy homes. It would be irresponsible for us to say you should completely ignore it, but you should know it's all hype. Just as your entire life can't be defined by your best and worst days, the value of your investments isn't determined by them either. Your job is to simply hold on for the ride and try your best to enjoy the view between the peaks and valleys. Don't pat yourself on the back when things go remarkably well, and don't shoot yourself in the foot when things are going poorly.

- **Take calculated risks.** As you accumulate more wealth, you're in a better position to take on more risk. This means investment opportunities such as cryptocurrencies, IPOs, and individual stock holdings can and should occupy a greater percentage of your total wealth. As we explained in chapter 3, once your income has fulfilled its purpose of providing flexibility, a good rule of thumb is to begin allocating 5 percent of your net worth to invest in emerging or riskier asset classes. This approach to diversification can accelerate you into financial independence sooner, and from there you have the option to reallocate even further.

# richuals

- **Think of investing like financial hygiene.** Consistency matters. If you're a reasonably clean person, it's safe to assume you wake up and brush your teeth and perform a long list of other grooming habits. Sure, on occasion you may forget or be unable to do one or the other, but in general you consistently clean your teeth in addition to other important parts of your body. You need to build the same degree of consistency with the act of investing. It's tempting to assume that you don't have to do this throughout the year because you will do it at the end of the year, but imagine if you did that with your teeth? Imagine if instead of brushing twice a day, you decided to give yourself a really good deep cleaning and flossing when you thought it mattered the most. Not only would that be painful, but you might risk losing a few teeth along the way.

  **If you're an employee and have access to a tax-deferred retirement account . . .**

- Seek to invest in your company's retirement plan in low-cost index funds.

- At a minimum, invest up to the amount the company is matching, particularly if the company is matching 100 percent (or dollar for dollar).

**If you're self-employed . . .**

- **Consider working with a CPA to open your own IRA or enroll in a 401(k) plan.** While there may not be a match, you are still able to deduct contributions from your taxable income. In some cases, you're able to make both employee and employer contributions, which allow you to invest considerably more over time. At a minimum, you should review opportunities to invest on a quarterly basis. If you can, we highly recommend opening a separate brokerage account that also allows you to invest anytime you want outside the restrictions and limits that come with an employer.

**In either case, remember:** *When it comes to investing, time in the market matters way more than timing.* Investing should be a recurring part of your life. It doesn't matter if one day you have $100, $1,000, or only $50. By building the habit and maintaining a constant mindfulness of your investments, you will ensure steady growth and be able to build considerable wealth over time.

- **Give yourself one less thing to think about; you deserve it.** There is no shortage of things to think about in this day and age. If you're a working adult, before you head to your job, you will have likely taken a shower and thought about what to wear, what you'll eat for breakfast, what to watch or listen to, and whether to respond to any messages you might have received overnight. And by the time you get to work, you'll likely have hundreds of other decisions to make. In addition, according to the Yankelovich marketing firm, the average person is exposed to approximately two thousand to four thousand ads on a daily basis.[5]

  It's no wonder we're all so tired or willing to procrastinate investing for our future. From your phone, social media platforms, billboards, print media, signage, and commercials, thousands of dollars are being spent to get you to do something at every turn. On the other hand, all of this spending can be viewed as an indicator of a thriving economy. Conceptually, companies believe they will get a return on their advertising investment; otherwise, they wouldn't be doing it. For you, as an index fund investor, give yourself one less thing to think about by assuring you have a slice of that pie.

  The last thing you probably want to do after a long day is to think about analyzing financial reports or whether your adviser is working in your best interest. By embracing the idea of index fund investing, you can rest comfortably knowing that you own a little slice of it all and that you'll ultimately earn your fair share of the pie.

# CHAPTER 8

# The He Said/She Said Dance

E very couple has an example of a shared experience where one person remembers the event happening one way and the other remembers it differently. Well, the story of our first conversation (and argument) about money is one of those cases. It's a classic he said/she said story, so we're sharing both versions. Don't worry, you don't have to choose sides. Later in this chapter, you'll learn how to talk to your partner about money and what to do if you've been in a pattern of avoiding money conversations with your loved ones.

## He Said

### "If I Knew You Had Credit Card Debt, I Never Would Have Dated You."

Kiersten and I were in the thick of the honeymoon phase. Our nights and weekends were filled with laughter, fancy dinners, cocktails, and passion. And as if that weren't enough, we were also co-workers, so our days included awkward attempts to conceal what was clearly the worst-kept secret in the office. During meetings, we'd exchange glances whenever someone made a comment that reminded us of a moment we shared. She'd raise her eyebrows and I'd tilt my head to the side trying not to bust out in laughter. Afterward, we'd go back to one of our desks and crack up together. It was like a Black version of *The Office*, and we had an entire library of nonverbal "that's what she said" jokes.

We were so head over heels for each other that we booked a vacation to Panama within the first few months of meeting. We agreed to split the cost, but when we returned, I was ready to jump back into my regular life of budgeting and saving for the future. Meanwhile, Kiersten wanted to keep the party going. I'd never met anyone who wanted to celebrate the ending of a nine-day vacation. (Who does that?)

That was a huge red flag for me. Money had already been a contributing factor to a prior relationship ending, and I didn't want to repeat the mistakes of the past. Don't get me wrong, we were having a lot of fun together, but I was beginning to wonder if we were compatible. I grew up in a working-class, immigrant household. I was taught to cling to every dollar I had because there was no guarantee another was coming. I knew my budget the way most people know their Social Security number. I could tell you exactly how much I sent to my student loans every month down to the penny. I knew my mortgage payment, my home association fee, how much I paid for insurance, car note, phone bill, everything! These numbers were so ingrained in my mind that even in Panama, I found myself calculating the cost of our meals one day and noticing that it was about what I'd spent on groceries for an entire month!

Kiersten, on the other hand, didn't have these hang-ups. If my childhood was a Jamaican episode of *Good Times*, hers was *The Cosby Show*. She never had to worry about making ends meet the way I did. Even as an adult, she found that earning money came naturally to her, and she was used to spending it however she wanted. Me? I always had to fight for it. When it came to money, she didn't sweat the details at all, and while I liked that (sometimes), I wasn't sure if it would work in a long-term relationship.

So, I invited her over so I could explain how I was feeling.

We started talking, and I could tell she wasn't really understanding where we were going. So I pulled up my spreadsheets and showed her all the records I'd kept of my financial life. I had folders of tax returns, Excel graphs, tables, and formulas I'd built to project the future value of my investments. I put it all out there! I browsed through some of my favorite online calculators, and I even introduced her to the online world of money blogs I was reading. I was showing her a side of me that I think she knew but didn't fully understand. And when I was done, she looked like a deer in headlights. It was clear she was uncomfortable talking about money like this, but I knew it was important. I was willing to be uncomfortable if it meant we could be real with each other.

Finally, after some awkward silence, she said, "I have bills too," and began randomly rattling them off. She revealed a little bit about her financial picture, but she wasn't going into nearly the level of detail I did. As she stumbled through her bills, I could feel a bomb about to drop. Then she said it.

"Well, I send $100 to American Express and about $75 to Visa every month." Then she listed a few other cards and some more cards . . . and more cards. I thought my head was going to explode. By the end, there were at least five revolving credit card balances in addition to a car loan, for a total debt balance of about $30,000. I didn't want to be right, but my suspicions were correct. The lifestyle she was living was way above what she could actually afford.

Every impromptu ATM visit, fancy dinner, extra round of cocktails, the random sets of shoes in the trunk of her car, and the lightly used gadgets lying around her apartment were all paid for with credit, and she had no plan to pay it off. She was flying by the seat of her pants under the assumption that one day a magical lump sum of money would fall in her lap and she'd be able to make it all disappear. But what upset me the most was knowing our vacation to Panama added to this already growing mountain of debt. Even though we used miles and some points to make it more affordable, it still cost each of us well over $1,000 out of pocket. And while I was trying to figure out how to pay off my portion in full by the end of the month, she was just avoiding it. Debt was like the sun to her. She loved to bask in it, but she'd never look it straight in the eye.

In the heat of the moment, instead of offering support or

providing a recommendation, I strung together one of the harshest collections of words I'd ever told anyone face-to-face. I wish I hadn't said it, but I straight up told her, "If I knew you had credit card debt, I never would have dated you." I think I wanted to say, "I wouldn't have gone on vacation with you," but for some reason I went for the jugular. Honestly, I think I really just wanted to talk about how uncomfortable our differences made me and I used this particular difference to shine a light on all of it.

I wanted Kiersten to know how seriously I took managing my money and that being with someone who didn't manage her money responsibly was a problem. I also wanted her to know that as much as I enjoyed having fun, planning for my future was equally important. I was financially preparing to take care of my mother, while Kiersten would likely inherit wealth from her parents. I thought she'd understand that I didn't like knowing our trip added to what was clearly a spending problem. Instead, all she heard was rejection and regret for all the good times we'd spent together. It was as if I threw every moment we'd ever shared together in the trash, all because I discovered she had credit card debt.

"Do you really mean that?" she asked me.

"Yeah, I do."

In that moment I knew whatever we had was done. She'd given me an opportunity to take it back, and I dug my heels further in the ground. I told myself I was making the smart decision by running from a ticking time bomb before it exploded. I basically made her the hopeless villain and cast myself as the morally superior hero defending the sacred laws of personal finance. And that was it. She grabbed her stuff and left.

## She Said

### *"I Was More Embarrassed That I Had Opened My Heart to a Man Who Refused to Compromise Than I Was About Having Debt."*

The day I met Julien, I knew he was special. My stomach did the wobble as soon as he walked into the room. We became fast friends due to our habit of swapping stories and jokes throughout the day. Our colleagues would hear us clowning and gather around us as we became the unofficial hosts of the secret Black people meeting that inevitably happens after the real meeting. Our relationship was lighthearted and fun.

I remember the first time he ever called me. He was pissed about something stupid at work and wanted to know if I felt the same way. I didn't but I said I did just to keep him talking. What can I say? I'm a people pleaser. Plus, he had one of those soothing radio voices like the kind you hear emceeing the quiet storm. I could listen to him all night. It took only a few more conversations with him to know that we saw and reacted to the world differently. We were opposites, but the dynamic felt familiar because my parents are, too, and their upbringings were also drastically different.

My father has a rebellious spirit. He's a notorious rule

breaker who raised me to think for myself and be a leader. Meanwhile, my mother is a pious woman who learns all the rules and finds comfort in their existence. Nothing is more important to her than God, and as a child I spent several days a week in church learning powerful spiritual concepts about faith and prosperity. Despite my parents being so different, being raised by them was a gift. It created an unusual combination that made me feel as if I could have everything I wanted without ever worrying about how I was going to get it.

When Julien and I first started dating, we spent all our time in my fancy midtown apartment because Julien never invited me to his house. I didn't mind because that made it easy for me to fold him into my social circle and introduce him to my alter ego.

Listen, back then, after work, I was the carefree girl who bought rounds of drinks for strangers, danced like everyone was watching, and cackled loudly when something was funny. It was all new to Julien and he was kinda standoffish, but I chalked it up to his being from Brooklyn. *He's just skeptical of everything and everybody!* I thought.

When he suggested we go on a vacation to Panama, honestly I was shocked. He didn't mean Panama City, Florida; he was talking about Panama-Panama! I agreed to go, and for nine days I scuttled around the hotel room trying to choreograph my farts and not be too messy. It was an incredible trip, but when we returned to Atlanta, I could tell things were off. I couldn't figure out what changed, but I needed to fix it.

I asked Julien what was wrong, not knowing he was going to unload on me. But before I knew it, we were sharing details about our life I wasn't prepared for. Then he told me that if he knew I had credit card debt, he wouldn't have dated me. It was as if all the air were sucked out of the room. I even gave him a chance to take it back by asking, "Do you really mean that?" and he said he did. The damage was done.

The thing is, I was comfortable with my money secrets. I knew debt wasn't a good thing, but I was in my twenties, having fun, and I'd always been able to earn more when I needed to. Plus, I'd experienced some devastating losses in my life, so I wasn't about to miss out on making amazing memories with the people I cared about just because I didn't have all the money I needed at the moment. That's literally what credit cards are for! I lived big, I loved big, I spent big, I gave big. I'm from Texas . . . that's what we do!

I just assumed having debt was normal, not a character flaw or something that couldn't be fixed when I felt like it. When Julien said he would never have dated me if he knew I had debt, it was as if the rose-colored glasses I was wearing came flying off and I immediately regretted revealing the parts of myself that weren't perky. I should have been mad, but I was more embarrassed that I had opened my heart to a man who refused to compromise than I was about having debt.

I didn't want to cry in front of him. I wanted to run away and hide, so I did. I gathered my things, I left, and our relationship ended that day.

They say hindsight is twenty-twenty for a reason. I look back now and wonder how in the hell I missed it. When he would tell me stories about growing up surrounded by gangs and violence, what was I thinking? When he talked about surviving walks to school in the mornings, what on earth was I hearing? I had a romanticized view of his struggle because I hadn't gone through it myself. In my eyes, his hardships were "worth it" because of who he became. To me, his experiences made him the man I had fallen in love with—resilient, practical, and witty enough to navigate unfamiliar environments—but I ignored his looming fear that it could all be taken away. I classified his stories as "inspiring" because it was easier than accepting how often the world is unfair and unaccommodating to good people.

In my family and the communities that I lived in, I saw plenty of examples of healthy marriages and long-term relationships. Both of my parents had long, successful careers that afforded both me and my older brother a constant sense of security. For me, spending money was simply a part of how relationships, families, and marriages were built and maintained. It was the glue.

Enough time has passed that I can say I appreciate the argument Julien and I had because it forced us to have uncomfortable conversations early in our relationship. Once we realized how much our histories with money shaped our identities, our beliefs about money became a welcome third wheel in our relationship.

I remember the day we made up. Julien hugged me and said, "One day, you are going to look back and laugh at the fact that you were crying over such an insignificant amount of money." Well, that day hasn't happened yet, but I do take comfort in reminding him how he almost missed out on the best thing that has ever happened to him over such an "insignificant amount of money."

## We Both Said

Now, even though we told you not to pick sides, it's natural to hear our story and immediately begin to choose a side you can best identify with. But our disagreement wasn't as simple as labeling any one person right or wrong, winner or loser. We can joke about it now, but at the time it was devastating, and we both believed it was a point of no return. After a few weeks, calmer heads prevailed, and we gave each other an opportunity to make the case for our respective point of view. Our hope in sharing our story is that you use our experience to see what's possible on the other side of conflict.

While we'd known each other for only a few months at the time, we brought decades of beliefs, behaviors, cultural idioms, insecurities, desires, and fears to the table that day. Kiersten was deep in her second decade of managing money with the rules she'd been given verbally or intuitively from well-meaning adults. Meanwhile, Julien was a little older and had spent almost thirty years on the edge of financial insecurity. He didn't grow up in a two-parent or two-income household and was just beginning to experience his first taste of financial flexibility. Considering the environment that he grew up in, he was so accustomed to extreme conflict in his life that he'd grown insensitive to minor disagreements.

Without this clashing of perspectives and a shared desire

to overcome them, we wouldn't have learned so much about ourselves or been able to share the lessons with each other. Considering money affects every aspect of our lives, it only made sense that making shared financial decisions became fertile ground for conflict.

As your life becomes more intertwined with someone else's, you'll be forced to confront your respective belief systems, and that includes your thoughts about money. Instead of teaching you how to fight, we want to help you normalize and navigate these conflicts so that you can unearth the jewels that lie beneath the surface. Disagreements about money aren't something to be afraid of; they're a natural by-product of growth.

## The Music We Heard

Dr. Sue Johnson is a clinical psychologist who specializes in emotionally focused therapy. She says that when couples fight (regardless of the topic), they're doing a dance. One partner makes a move, and the other one responds accordingly. She insists the dance is always the problem—not you, not me, not us—and not the topic. By focusing on the dance, we can shift our focus and look at our *interaction patterns* whenever there's an issue. The rhythm of one person responding to the other person's moves is what ultimately defines the dance, and our ability to instinctively know when to reach out and grab the other's hand for a spin requires what Dr. Johnson calls emotional attunement.

If the conflict is the dance itself, think of your emotions as the music. Being emotionally attuned means you can both

CONFLICT = DANCE

hear the same song, or at the very least can acknowledge that yours isn't the only one playing. In other words, it's not enough to just go through the moves together if one of you is grooving to Barry White and the other is swinging to Barry Manilow.

When you've been in a pattern of avoiding conversations with your partner about money, it's as if you've both been attending a silent disco. Everyone's dancing, but you can't hear any music. If you want to get attuned, it's important to understand what unresolved money arguments sound like, emotionally speaking.

## 1 | *Name-Calling: Conversations About Spending*

Over the years, we've met and spoken with hundreds of couples about money, and the most common argument we've heard is about spending. Latoya wants to know why her partner has more shoes than an NBA locker room, while Ricky wants to know why his front door has more boxes than an Amazon warehouse four days a week. In most cases, it's clear that one person dragged the other to us because they needed them to understand something. They'll say, "Y'all can explain it better than I can," or, "Every time I try, it just goes in one ear and out the other." It always reminds us of frustrated pet owners bringing Roscoe to a dog whisperer because nothing they've tried has worked: Roscoe just keeps peeing on the couch.

Almost without fail, as they're detailing the scene of the conflict, someone says something along the lines of "one of us is the saver and the other is the spender." The premise is rooted in the assumption that the saver is the good guy, the responsible one, the one who makes the best or better decisions about money. On the other hand, the spender is the bad guy, the irresponsible one who always gets it wrong and needs to be fixed.

For starters, we're not relationship police doling out punishment to people who overspend at the mall. Second, we disagree with any framing that locks people into fixed financial identities. Those labels are just that—labels. And no single label can fully encapsulate anyone's identity because in reality *everyone spends*.

The idea of "savers" and "spenders" is simple, convenient, and easy to remember, but it is not a reflection of the world we live in. Saving and spending are fluid concepts. The only difference between savers and spenders is the time horizon. Spenders are spending for today, and savers are setting aside money to spend in the future. For example, if we save $20,000 in one year to buy a car with cash, and then we spend that $20,000 the following year to get it, are we savers or spenders? It depends on what year you ask us, right?

Getting attuned starts with freeing your relationship from the constraints of labels, and it's the first step to inviting curiosity back into your conversations. Whenever you're having a conversation about spending, you need to go into it acknowledging that there are no villains. Your ability to have a nonjudgmental conversation about money requires swapping the paradigm from "good or bad" to "now or later." Whenever anybody spends money, they're chasing a feeling, and the goal of the conversation is to find out what it is. Whether it's wanting to feel security, spontaneity, or pleasure, once you acknowledge that both you and your partner want the same thing—to feel something—the nature of the conversation becomes less about the spender/saver persona you've assigned each other and more about looking at the decision objectively and finding new, creative ways to reach the goal.

> *Getting attuned starts with freeing your relationship from the constraints of labels, and it's the first step to inviting curiosity back into your conversations.*

Couples usually describe their goal as getting on the same page, but it's important to go much deeper than that. The ultimate goal with your partner should be achieving a state of harmony, where each person is allowed to express themselves fully in a way that contributes to your collective sound.

## 2 | *Nagging: Conversations About Saving*

Not only does nagging strain a relationship, but it's also guaranteed to put someone on the defensive because of its persistence. Saving money is an ongoing part of managing your finances. Over time, constant panicky warnings that someone should be saving *more* erode the ability to look at any situation objectively. This level of surveillance makes sense in totalitarian governments, but in relationships it's conversational quicksand. The more you do it, the deeper you sink. All of a sudden, the reminders about money blend in with the daily chorus of other unsolicited prompts to wipe the counters down or take the trash out, and it all begins to sound like a broken record. If you don't get the tone right, at some point the person being nagged will start to think that your real beef is with them, and not about the money at all.

Attunement in this area boils down to classic reframing. As we mentioned, saving is just "planning to spend later," and guess what's more fun than talking about what we're *not* buying? Obsessing over buying it in the future!

Our tried-and-true advice for conversations about saving is to talk about your future plans. Meaningful conversations about future plans act like a release valve, giving a potentially high-pressure situation a chance to stabilize. Instead of saying,

"Babe, what's with all the Starbucks cups? We need to be saving, not slurping!" start your request with an "I" statement. That indicates you're participating in the conversation as a partner, not a parent. "I can't WAIT to upgrade our TV! I think I'm going to cut back on Chipotle and see what kind of dent that makes in our saving goal. Would you consider doing the same for Starbucks? I bet we could have the cash by November and catch a great deal instead of waiting."

Anticipation is a helluva drug, and there are positive psychological benefits when you look forward to something.[1] Optimism is more reliable than willpower when it comes to doing things you don't want to do. For instance, when we had to cut back on eating out to save up for a vacation, we would cook foods at home that were reflective of the local cuisine and play their local music to help set the scene. Sometimes we would even YouTube the destination and watch other people's experiences and anticipate what we were looking forward to most. Not only were these small rewards a welcome distraction from another night in, but they also helped us become more disciplined.

*Optimism is more reliable than willpower when it comes to doing things you don't want to do.*

## 3 | *Blaming: Conversations About Debt*

It's pretty common for one partner to owe more than the other, and that disparity can lead to feelings of resentment and insecurity. Constant reminders about how much debt somebody brings to a relationship, as well as the approach they use to tackle it, can be a source of tension. The person with the debt may feel a deep sense of shame from believing their debt means they are wrong or bad. On the flip side, the person without debt can feel obligated to help pay for it, which can create resentment. Trying to dance to a song that's composed of shame and obligation is like trying to waltz to "Cotton-Eyed Joe."

For Kiersten, the shame surrounding her debt triggered defensiveness. She'd mastered her ability to use religious platitudes whenever she didn't know the answer to something. She was also accustomed to avoiding conflict in other areas of her life and had learned to live among her problems, instead of trying to solve them. From that emotional vantage point, that initial confrontation about debt felt like a personal attack. And to her credit, it was.

For us, attunement in this particular area required letting go. Kiersten needed to let go of any romantic notions of being rescued, and Julien needed to let go of his judgment. We both needed to let go of popular debt-payoff plans that treated debt as a moral failing, and learned how to strike a balance where frugality and flexibility could coexist. And once we teamed up, combined our finances, and started to pay off our debt together, we became critical of the social and cultural norms that created it to begin with. We learned to dance together.

Our approach worked really well for us, but there are legitimate reasons to tackle your debts separately, like eligibility restrictions on forgiveness plans or just personal preference. In those cases, you can agree that each person is responsible for their debt and that you won't ever co-sign for loans together unless you both benefit from it equally. Either way is fine as long as you remember that regardless of the path you choose, emotional attunement still makes it a highly coordinated effort where both people contribute to its massive success or its failure.

## Say "Tell Me More"

In any money conversation you're having, use the phrase "tell me more" as a way to indicate when you don't understand your partner or need more context. It's like conversational lube that keeps us talking longer. Saying "tell me more" is not as harsh as asking "why?" and not as dismissive as saying "no." It's a signal that more context is needed and follow-up questions will allow a better understanding of the other person's perspective.

Judgment and harsh language are the equivalent of placing your finger on a vinyl-record player in the middle of your dance. That sharp and sudden scratch completely wrecks the flow and puts a halt to the conversation. Instead, saying "tell me more" is a gentler nudge, inviting the other person to continue expressing themselves and feel encouraged to take a conversational risk. Think of it as a volume adjuster or equalizer so you can listen to your partner more effectively.

Now, it's important to know that tone matters here. When using "tell me more," the emphasis is on the "more" and not the "tell." Think of the last time you wanted more of something because you were enjoying it. That's what you're aiming for. Don't go full-blown Girl 6. The phrase should definitely sound more like a request and not a demand.

## One Caveat to "Tell Me More"

There is one important caveat you should know when using "tell me more" in charged situations. It is impossible to feel curious and inquisitive while you also feel threatened and intimidated. After the first argument, it took awhile for one of us (ahem, Julien) to regain the other's trust related to sharing financial details. For a long time, one of us (ahem, Kiersten) would cry every time we talked about money because she was overwhelmed and replaying "if I had known, I never would have dated you" in her head, among other things. In those moments, Julien wasn't blasting Kiersten with the phrase like a fire extinguisher. In fact, using "tell me more" in times like those can do more harm than good and serves to undermine its future use. In those hotbed moments, good old-fashioned patience tends to work best. Instead of forcing a flammable conversation, you're better off preserving the dance floor for future use.

# The 51 Percent Rule

The Greek philosopher Heraclitus once said, "No man steps in the same river twice, for it's not the same river and he's not the same man." This is what it feels like to manage conflict in a relationship. Attunement is always in a state of flux because your partner is always experiencing new things that shape how they think. Keeping up with all of it is hard. And honestly, it's work. But when you're in a mature relationship, you are agreeing to hang in there while the other person figures it out and hoping they grant the same grace to you.

There's a saying in the personal finance community that most money arguments aren't about money, and we've found that to be largely true. In the beginning of our relationship, we used to think all our financial arguments were the result of not having enough money. We figured that once we had more of it, all our money issues would magically disappear and we'd be on the same page till death do us part. Nothing would be further from the truth. As the late, great Notorious B.I.G. said, "Mo money, mo problems." Over time, we would learn that earning more income may ease the stress of the decision-making process, but it doesn't make the difficult decisions go away. In other words, conflict was a constant presence in our life that ebbed and flowed as time went on.

In the three years we spent dating, we learned how to fight fair about money through having lots of conflict. But preparing for marriage brought on new challenges as we began to talk about higher-stakes decisions like estate planning and supporting our parents. We were haunted by the statistics we

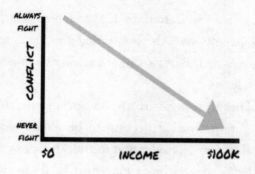

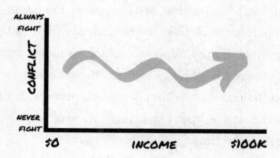

were finding about marriages, money, and divorce. According to the American Psychological Association, about 50 percent of marriages end up in divorce, and disagreements about money are the leading reason.[2]

Knowing this, we made it our focus to improve the odds by taking money issues off the table and deciding that if we were going to get divorced, it was going to be because of the second or third most popular reason—anything but number one!

Although we had been practicing productive financial conversations for several years, we still lacked the wisdom and perspective that come from decades of interactions. Luckily, Kiersten's parents have been married for more than forty years, and her dad, Blue, is full of backwoods one-liners and poetic advice.

One of his greatest hits is "the 51 percent rule." It's simple: everyone gets married expecting to be happy most of the time, but they don't consider that technically speaking "most" is only 50 + 1—hence the 51 percent rule. It's his way of reminding couples to lower their unrealistic expectations and to see marriage, like investing, as a long game. Periods of 80 percent happiness can be followed by periods of only 20 percent happiness due to grief, illness, missteps, or mourning. When things get rocky, he reminds us that we're shooting for 51 percent and the real work is simply making peace with the existence of the other 49 percent, because none of us is entitled to happiness all the time.

Well, Blue wouldn't say it quite like that. He'd say something like "Y'all ain't been 'round the cup long enough to find the handle." In other words, we haven't been married long enough to complain about anything. And because life's highs and lows are so fluid, there's little value in keeping score.

There were several seasons within our financial journey where we weren't "happy." Our aggressive saving plan in our early years meant missing out on activities we could do and delaying a lot of purchases we could afford, like much-needed home repairs that would've made life more comfortable. We didn't enjoy stepping over musty towels in our living room from a leak in the foundation or missing the milestone-birthday celebrations of our loved ones. We didn't enjoy driving in Atlanta heat with the windows down because we didn't feel like spending the money to repair the car's air-conditioning. But having gone through it, we now recognize that happiness alone is a low bar, especially when humbled, grateful, and content are options.

*We now recognize that happiness alone is a low bar, especially when humbled, grateful, and content are options.*

OUR DECISION TO TAKE THE leading cause of divorce off the table might not have been the most romantic one, but it has certainly given us the emotional and financial capacity to deal with any of the other issues as they arise. Marriage is hard, and relationships require work. It becomes increasingly more difficult when you add high-stress jobs, parenting, caring for aging parents, and any other pressures life may place at your doorstep.

There are no easy answers when it comes to relationships and money. There's a reason why there are so many books, counselors, workshops, seminars, and reality television shows out there dedicated to the subject. But as we alluded to in chapter 2, being rich and regular is ultimately about asking yourself, "Which work do I want to do?"

# rule

- **Happiness is not the goal.** The 51 percent rule doesn't mean that you are *un*happy 49 percent of the time; it simply acknowledges that there are a range of emotions in every marriage, and happiness is just one of them. In fact, studies have shown happiness is more strongly linked to genetics than external circumstances. Like fear, anxiety, thrill, or delight, happiness is among a wide range of biological reactions. The idea that we should pursue it at all times or that constant happiness can be achieved in any endeavor is unrealistic.

# richuals

- **Schedule short but frequent conversations.** For us, healthy and regular dialogue has been the most productive way we attune to each other and rebuild all the brain muscles lost to the busyness of an increasingly digital world. We schedule short, frequent conversations, and while one person talks, the other person's only job is to be an active listener.
- **Don't be afraid to press pause.** Whenever our conversations hit a dead end, we use a safe word that acts like a pause button. So if one of us started or ended a sentence with our safe word, it meant

that whatever we said was serious and should not be used as material for a punch line or repurposed for a future roast.

In money conversations, using a safe word means you've hit a wall and you're committing to continue the conversation, at a later date. This temporary relief supports the process of emotional attunement and leaves space for healing.

# CHAPTER 9

# Find Your
# FI Community

Want to know how to ruin your next Thanksgiving? Start on an ambitious journey to achieve financial independence and try to persuade your friends and family they should be doing the same! We know this because we've spoiled many a dinner, special occasion, and cocktail hour with the people we love the most. We've perfected the art of providing unsolicited countercultural financial advice at the absolute worst times. We've done it so many times it's hard to pick the best, or in this case worst, event we've ruined.

There was that one time at Kiersten's parents' home shortly after our son was born. Considering he was their first grandchild, they were over-the-top excited and keen on giving him toys—especially cars and trucks. But between the toy cars he already had, the new ones they bought him every time we came over, and the ride-on cars that arrived as gifts from our extended family in Texas, our tiny townhome had become a garage for his auto collection. So, being the purpose-driven and financially savvy family we are, we humbly requested a moratorium on all gift giving. And because that wasn't enough, for his first birthday, which we hosted at their home, we decided a simpler, more responsible approach would be to ask for contributions to his 529 plan in lieu of gifts.

Makes sense, right? He won't remember the toys he had as a toddler, everyone who contributes would receive an in-state tax deduction for their contribution, and as our son leaves the nest for college, he does so knowing that his village helped to get him there. We might've even thrown in a virtuous stat or two on how the excessive plastic and cardboard boxes the toys were wrapped in were harmful to the environment. We can't quite repeat all the words that were said to us in response to our well-intended recommendation, but the gist is that our young asses had no business telling their grown asses what to do with their money, especially not in their house. Furthermore, according to our parents, asking guests to contribute to our son's college education was tacky: a 529 contribution wasn't a gift; it was a donation.

There was also the time Julien's cousin, his wife, and their daughters came over to our home. We don't get to see them often so when we do, it's an all-out affair with food and fun times for our children to play together. While catching up, they shared some big news—that they'd both decided to go back to school to earn advanced degrees. They were excited but admittedly hesitant to share the news with us because they didn't want to feel judged. "We know how you guys feel about student loans," they said. This led to a heartbreaking and tense discussion about our future lives and respective abilities to spend time together as a family. Like us, they're a young family with plenty of life ahead of them. But somehow, our habit of openly sharing our beliefs about debt, money, and careers created a wedge between us.

We could go on and on. Some of the people closest to us have tried to hide their recent car purchases, home purchases, and lavish vacations from us. Over the years, we've purposely not been invited to celebrations because someone assumed attending wasn't in our budget. The absolute worst situations are friends who simply go radio silent. Years later, you discover that something like a blog post or reaction to something on social media made them feel as if we'd decided to take a different path in life—one that excluded them.

We're not alone in facing this weird sense of isolation from friends and family. In 2019, we met Joel, a young, talented videographer, and soon began collaborating with him on creative projects. Meeting us sparked an interest in him to explore his own spending habits, investing, and the role the two played in his ability to work on projects he cared about, not just on those that paid the bills.

One morning, out of the blue, Joel sent us a text message with a screenshot of his investment account showing his current net worth of $100,558. The corresponding text said, "I don't really have anyone to share this with so I figured I'd let you know. I woke up this morning to a $100K net worth. Been investing like 70% of everything since ya'll opened my eyes." We were over-the-moon excited about his progress but heartbroken that he didn't feel comfortable sharing his accomplishment with his loved ones even though, at the time, he was still living at home with his parents.

When you make the life-changing decision to cash out, you aren't just leaving a job behind. In some ways, it may feel as if you were leaving an entire community behind. You'll begin to feel as if people see you differently, and in some cases it's because they do.

In our case, we'd fallen into the trap of virtue signaling. When we shared how much we saved in a year, our net-worth gains, or our point of view on passive investing, it made people feel as if we weren't just better off but better than them. Our open displays of financial responsibility had somehow come across as moral superiority. And as tempting as it is to double down on those beliefs, doing so would serve only to create an even greater gap between us and the people we love.

To find the delicate, more satisfying balance between being radical and relatable, we leaned into the same insights we used whenever we had a disagreement as a couple—the 51 percent rule. We stopped expecting unconditional support 100 percent of the time and opened ourselves up to the range of emotions that long-term non-romantic relationships offer. We started to cherish belonging, connection, and tradition while still holding space for our love of challenging social norms and bucking the system. Instead of always leading conversations about money, we started to let our friends and family go first, and rather than offering unsolicited advice, we would ask if they wanted a second opinion. Most important, we stopped using their financial situation as a scoreboard for how much they valued our perspective. In any relationship, there will be good times and bad times. Our hope is that when it's all said and done, the former will outweigh the latter.

As you embark on your own cashing out journey, know that your friends and family may not be your most supportive community. Instead of trying to convert them, recognize they have their own set of emotional baggage and life experiences to sort through, and open yourself up to building new relationships with people all around the world who are also committed to cashing out.

Luckily, like every other fringe countercultural group, FI enthusiasts tend to flock together. There's an entire world of money nerds, groups, forums, and platforms for people at every stage of your journey—people who get excited at the thought of taking family vacations entirely paid for by credit card points, squeal upon hearing that the annual contribution limits of 401(k) plans have increased by $500, and don't cringe at the thought of doing taxes, budgeting, or digging into spreadsheets.

To scratch the community itch you may be looking for, not only do you need to look inward, but you need to look elsewhere. If you would've told us years ago that some of our best memories would be stargazing in the middle of the woods with a white family from Florida, we would've asked you to pass whatever strain you were smoking. But in hindsight we can say that as we found "our people," we also started redefining what it means to be "our people."

# "Our People"

The pressure to relate to your friends and family is more than just a matter of personal preference; it's an evolutionary trait. As human beings, we are biologically inclined to stick with whom we know or, as the old folks say, to "dance with the one who brought you." Our primitive brains still trick us into thinking our survival is at stake. However, social acceptance is no longer a life-or-death matter.

In fact, research suggests that familiarity may heighten feelings of impostor syndrome. Dr. Richard Gardner conducted a study on social support and "perceived impostorism." He found that people were more likely to feel like an impostor when they sought feedback from their in-group instead of when they requested opinions from people outside it.[1] To put it another way, it's fine to go to your family for some things, but if what you need is confidence, you may have to look for community elsewhere.

We routinely receive emails with subject lines like "Isolated millionaire in Atlanta" or "Young Black Male entering the World." While our Black readers and followers express deep gratitude for having found us, they also admit that their following of the movement is a guilty pleasure, because the financially independent community is predominantly white. The diversity (or lack thereof) in the FIRE community comes up a lot whenever we speak with press or Black podcast hosts. One particular interviewer summed it up perfectly, using an old southern saying to describe who we were to his audience: "Y'all are like flies in buttermilk."

There are plenty of reasons to not pursue financial freedom; being Black isn't one of them. While the prevalence of white men with high incomes in certain fields is true, the people we've met along the way have been timely reminders that sometimes the support you need can be found outside your immediate circle. When you can connect deeply with like-minded people, you get to come up with new ways to relate to yourself. You get to discover what you actually want without judgment and work toward creating it without fear of rejection.

Finding a community of people with financial philosophies that are in accord with yours will help you feel less like a weirdo for seeing the world the way you do. Going through the process of debt payoff and building wealth can be a lonely experience if you don't have folks in your corner who truly understand you.

Consider the role support groups play in helping people recover from an injury, bereavement, or trauma. While those may all sound extreme, you could make a case that the student loan crisis, the pending retirement crisis, and exposure to social oppression will all require some degree of mental and emotional support. Quite frankly, you could make the case that the constant barrage of advertising Americans are exposed to is a form of trauma, that the role work plays in our life is a form of addiction, and that our cultural tendency to spend more than we earn is a type of compulsive behavior. So having a community to help you heal and recover is an incredibly valuable tool on your journey to financial independence.

# Come for the Content,
# Stay for the Community

The FIRE community is unique in that it's a community of practice (CoP).[2] A CoP is defined as "a group of people who share a concern or passion for something they do, and learn how to do it better as they interact regularly."[3] In other words, the community functions like a fine wine or fancy cheese; it gets better with time.

A defining trait of communities of practice is that they keep a repository of resources. FIRE enthusiasts have been documenting their experiences, stories, tools, scripts, and approaches to problem solving for decades. From blogs, to books, to podcasts and even documentaries—it's literally all online, just out there, for free.

But content isn't community. This information continues to appreciate in value because of the comments and inquiries from others actively learning from it and contributing their own experiences, good and bad. That's why we advise people to come for the content but stay for the community. The math is the math, but the magic is in the community.

When we found the FIRE community, we were blown away at how willing they were to talk about the failures of the American Dream. When words failed, they were generous and directed us to endless numbers of databases, charts, and studies. When that wasn't enough, they hosted in-person meetups and camps that allowed for more nuanced conversations.

During our first visit to CampFI, we were invited as guest

speakers and jumped at the opportunity to meet other families on the same path we were. We were initially hesitant because the event was being held in rural Florida and we knew we would likely be the only Black people there. Furthermore, the message we planned to share with the audience shined a light on the racial wealth gap—an uncomfortable topic for a mainly white audience. However, to our surprise, the response was overwhelmingly positive, and we befriended several people from all walks of life. There, we truly learned the wider societal implications of the FIRE movement and how the shared values of the people in the community overshadowed our differences.

In a community of practice, there are no built-in assumptions about who can teach. When the learning is collaborative, we all benefit from the group's collective intelligence. The fact that you don't blog about health care doesn't stop us from learning from your experiences about purchasing insurance. Or just because you're not an accountant by trade doesn't mean we won't benefit from a walk-through of how you use Excel to create budgets. For example, one of our favorite talks was by Bradley Rice at CampFI, where he explained how his Salesforce expertise allows him to earn six figures a year working part time. We loved it because it was another reminder of how much our income options can improve once we let go of the idea of lifetime employment. Now he spends his days teaching others how they can become Salesforce professionals and change the trajectory of their earning at talentstacker.com.

While the individual emotional benefits of finding a supportive financial community are significant, the most valuable benefit is even simpler. It's a tactic that feels forgotten in today's culture, arguably a lost art form. It's something we teach our children to do but far too often fail to exhibit as adults. It's the natural by-product of community, and it's called sharing.

You're probably too old to remember being scolded by a parent or guardian for not sharing, but chances are it happened to you. Unfortunately, as we grow older, the importance of sharing is deprioritized in favor of other virtues like honesty, professionalism, and a strong work ethic. But imagine if that wasn't the case. Imagine if we de-compartmentalized sharing and allowed it to spill into broader areas of our lives.

A few years after we'd moved into our new home, we decided it was finally time to make some upgrades to improve the way it functioned. In the process of purchasing and installing new furniture, we made the decision to buy a new set of tools. Recalling the last time we needed to install furniture, we knew that not having quality tools added hours of time and hand and back pain to the process. But while we took pride in our ability to afford our new power drill, we couldn't help but think we'd probably use it only a few times a year and certainly wouldn't use every attachment that came with it. In that moment, we realized that if we'd simply had a better, deeper relationship with our neighbors, we could've asked to borrow their toolbox, which they would've gladly given us.

In America, we all call where we live a community, but we rarely act like one in the purest sense. We willingly pay a home association fee to cover the cost of the entry gate, pool, clubhouse, landscaping, exteriors, and insurance. We all also claim to take pride in our neighborhood and want to keep it clean and safe. But our desire to share stops at the exterior walls. The moment we're inside, all sharing ceases.

Even though we all probably use toilet paper, have similar entertainment tastes, and rely on the same kitchen staples, we don't ever share any of those things with each other. The thought of buying in bulk to share with a neighbor or carpooling or ringing a neighbor's doorbell because you're one egg short to make a batch of cookies seems like a scene from an old television show: not real life. Sure, there are people who share Netflix passwords and people who are on a family cable/internet plan, but overall sharing has been completely nixed from American culture in favor of individualism and convenience.

The FI community, at large, willingly embraces sharing as a lever to accelerate financial independence. When we were looking for low-cost party ideas for our son's second birthday, people generously offered recommendations. When we were looking for local getaways within driving distance of our home, other couples provided tips and itineraries. In some cases, they'd even share a promotional code to earn us a free appetizer, discounted ticket, or free trial of a service. All of these seemingly small acts of kindness added up to big savings over time and contributed to our achieving our financial goals.

Another benefit of belonging to a finance community: you start to build deep relationships with people based on shared values that transcend race, religion, sexual orientation, nationality, political affiliation, or any other aspect of life that far too often divides us.

For instance, when we visit the United Kingdom, we know we can reach out to our friends Ken and Mary of thehumble penny.com, who achieved financial independence at the age of thirty-four. Though thousands of miles away, they were two of the very first people we met online after sharing our story, and they instantly made us feel like welcome members of the family.

Similarly, if we ever wanted to explore living internationally, we could get advice from Amon and Christina of ourrichjourney.com. They have lived in California, Japan, and Portugal and achieved financial independence at thirty-nine. After years of frugal living, working as expats, and investing at a high rate, they purchased and renovated a gorgeous villa with an orchard where they grow their own organic fruits and vegetables.

## Ways to Find Your People

When our son transitioned into his pre-K class, he had to make an entirely different set of friends. The first week, he'd come home grumpy and restless because nobody wanted to play with him. At first, it was heartbreaking to hear him so upset by his inability to make new connections, so we'd coddle him with hugs, kisses, and a few jelly beans after school. But then we realized he needed to learn how to make friends and that it was our job to give him the tools to make this process easier.

There's a good chance you're not a toddler, but the fact is, even adults struggle with making new friends, and we've found it can be a huge obstacle along the journey. So here are the best ways to meet your new money besties.

## 1 | *Online*

Online is by far the easiest, most frictionless way to meet people also on the cashing out journey, especially if you use social media. You can search the hashtags #financialindependence, #debtfreecommunity, and #financialfreedom and stumble upon hundreds of thousands of individual posts from people on the same path as you.

Social media platforms are also home to several groups you can join, usually for free. These groups can be organized by topic (for example, FI, Debt Freedom, Cheap Meals) or by demographic (Mothers, Women, Women of Color, LGBTQ+, and so on) or even by lifestyle (Single, Socially Conscious, Military, and so forth). You can find a few of our favorites on Facebook, like "Women of Color Pursuing FI," "Women's Personal Finance (Women on FIRE)," and "ChooseFI." Joining an active group ensures you always have money-related content on your primary feed or timeline because someone is always asking a question. And because these conversations are threaded, you can see many different perspectives on one topic.

But as with all things, there is a downside to social community, and the most common problem with these groups is dealing with the varying degrees of knowledge. One day you may be privy to the ins and outs of how to navigate a backdoor

Roth IRA from someone who has done it for years. The next day the group may be flooded with questions about more fundamental financial topics. In most cases, the admins for these groups are volunteers and will moderate discussions for abuse but not for knowledge level or even truth. You'll need to be discerning about the advice you take and cautious about how you engage with strangers.

Another option is to join a paid community that requires a monthly or annual fee. These types of communities typically offer value-adds like access to unique content, guest speakers, and more curated topic selection. It's still not an internet utopia, but the likelihood that you'll be surrounded by like-minded people is much higher in a paid community than in the open-to-the-public groups.

## 2 | *Podcasts*

Personal finance podcasts changed the way we talked about money. When you listen to other people's stories, successes, and failures, your perception of what is possible for you changes. Plus, podcasts are a great way to find other voices and personalities. Naturally, when you follow or subscribe to their work, you'll inevitably be led to others just like them.

One of our favorites is *Journey to Launch* by Jamila Souffrant. She's a married mother of three, based out of New York City, and, like us, she was drawn to the financial independence movement as a pathway to improve her quality of life. In fact, our very first interview, shortly after we launched our blog, was on her podcast.

*Popcorn Finance* by Chris Browning is another of our favorites, especially if you're busy. Chris's goal is to give you a kernel of financial information in the amount of time it takes to make a bag of popcorn. So even if you're just taking a walk or have a short commute, there's no excuse to avoid learning more about money.

### 3 | *In Person*

The value you can gain from in-person interactions is unmatched. Something that started as simple as an email and an invite to coffee has led us on adventures where we're sitting on the sidelines of an Atlanta United soccer game, chopping it up about money.

But beyond one-on-one interactions, there are two predominant types of in-person meetups for the financial independence community: free and paid.

Free meetups tend to be smaller and more informal, kind of like study groups in college. They're usually in public spaces like a brewery or a coffee shop, and the agenda is loose. Sometimes there's a general topic the group will discuss, like real estate. Other times there is no topic, and you operate in the same way you would in a networking event at work: introduce yourself, ask people about their story, and see if you have anything in common. Some free meetups are far more structured, like mini TED talks where an expert speaks and then opens up the floor for conversation. In our experience, the more informal these are, the better. The lack of formality makes the entire experience more relaxing and takes the pressure off any insecurities you may have about money. Events like these are typically promoted online, through social media and the blogs, podcasts, and video channels of your favorite personal finance personalities.

The paid events are more curated and spread over a few days, like CampFI or the EconoMe Conference. We like these because they're longer, which gives us more time to get to know people. Because we're a money-conscious crew, other attendees typically go out of their way to lower the costs of lodging by offering roommate sign-ups and carpool options. A quick search on any of the online forums for the specific event will allow you to see threads of other people who are planning to attend. If you don't see any, you can always start one.

The best part about paid events is the format. While the keynote speeches form the foundation of the agenda, the event coordinators usually leave lots of free time. The first time we attended an event, we were unaware and used the empty time to go back to our hotel room. But by day two, we realized it was intentional and made more of an effort to connect with people and went to attendee-led breakouts, where the topics can range anywhere from side hustling to real estate investing to health care and general budget management.

As scary as it may sound, finding the courage to attend in-person events is one of the best investments you can make in your financial future. In fact, our very first in-person event was a millionaire meetup, and it did not disappoint. We were sitting around a fire in a hotel courtyard in Dallas, surrounded by dozens of millionaires and aspiring millionaires. Naturally, we were drawn to one of the organizers of the session who was a Black woman. She stood up and introduced herself, saying, "Hi, my name is Phylecia. I live in Denver, Colorado, my net worth is $875,000, and I am financially independent." It was the first time we'd ever heard someone state their net worth out loud in person, and it made us feel less isolated in our beliefs.

#### 4 | *Online/In-Person Combination*

We've met people like Phylecia and Bradley only a handful of times in real life, but we've been able to keep up with them over the years thanks to the internet. We follow each other on social media channels, and we've been able to support and encourage each other when needed. Meeting people in real life and then continuing a relationship online has been our preferred approach to building community. It has removed the constraints associated with formal learning and allows us to access resources whenever our phone is nearby. We can't begin to tell you how often we've sent quick DMs or pings to ask for recommendations or double-check an approach.

While it isn't possible (or suggested) to follow every person you meet online, it's the best way to immerse yourself in money-smart principles and ensure they stick. So much of what we consider "normal" is based entirely on what our current group of friends or family is doing. When you incorporate new people into your social media feed, it shows you what a rich life actually looks like. You become less swayed by how the media portrays "rich" and more convinced about what's possible for you.

## Last Word on Community

Beyond just serving the individual, the purpose of community is ultimately to improve neighborhoods, advance social justice causes, and influence better policies in government. Remember when we said we were making home improvements? Well, one of those improvements was to purchase a freezer for our garage. Our thinking was, the more we cooked in batches and froze our meals, the less time we'd spend cooking and the less money we'd spend on food.

Before we went freezer shopping, we asked our community for tips on what to look for. In seconds, we were flooded with recommendations. We were so grateful that when we made the decision to purchase our freezer, we decided to buy two—one for us and another for someone who could really use it. Again, we asked our online community to nominate someone who was deserving, and almost instantly they pointed us to Erica "Umi" Clahar.

Erica ran a local Atlanta nonprofit called Umi Feeds where she rescued food from local restaurants and served it to people in need. Having a freezer would allow her to store more food and ultimately serve more families. So that's what we did. We bought one small five-cubic-foot freezer for our garage and funded the purchasing of a fourteen-and-a-half-cubic-foot freezer for her organization. The timing couldn't have been better, because at the time we were in the middle of a global pandemic and several families were in desperate need of delicious and nutritious meals. Our intention was to help one family, but our community directed us on how we could help hundreds more. If it weren't for them, we likely would never have heard of Erica or the amazing work she's doing right in our own backyard.

The point is, you don't have to cash out alone. The more you give and the more you share, the more likely you'll make new friends in unexpected places who will gladly support you along the way. They may not look like you, share your accent, or be the same age, but they certainly won't look at you as if you were crazy for wanting to live a frugal, unconventional, and generous life. They'll hold you accountable if you stray from your goals or values, and they'll celebrate like hell when you crush them.

In the meantime, your family and friends may still be on their own respective paths. You will have achieved the improbable, and you might be tempted to say, "See . . . I told you so." In those moments, our advice is—don't.

## rules

- **Give yourself more credit.** The desire to have full, unbridled support from family and friends is natural. Consequently, it can be heartbreaking when the people you expect to support you express doubt, concern, or explicitly warn against a decision you're making. More often than not, these expressions are a fear-based response that is rooted in their desire to protect you from failure. What feels like a lack of support can actually be an expression of their love. In those moments, give yourself more credit and ensure your own voice is the one you trust the most.

- **Don't judge a book by its color.** While there's comfort to be found in the familiarity of one's cultural or ethnic groups, you shouldn't limit or exclude the possibility of building valuable relationships with people who are outside the group(s) you identify with. Many of the people we've leaned on and have helped us aren't Black but have similar shared interests and viewpoints as ours.

## richuals

- **Demote your gurus.** Sometimes you can learn more valuable life, business, and career lessons from small-business owners, entrepreneurs, and leaders in your local community than the gurus on television and social media. Use the big names to introduce you to new ideas, but don't aim to mimic them. Rather, you should look to emulate the actions of the people who are bringing these ideas to life wherever you are.

- **Become a connector.** Keep your friends and family in mind as you come across different personalities, experiences, and tips from within the community. As you find content that may be relevant to them, share it without attaching yourself to whether they use it. Keep in mind that changing a perspective is usually a game of inches. A simple "this made me think of you" goes a long way.

- **YMMV (your mileage may vary).** You know how car commercials add this disclaimer to indicate that results may be different for every driver? The same is true for financial independence. Because community members can be so vocal about their experience, it's easy to fall into the trap of comparison. Get into the practice of being inspired by who people are on the inside, and not what they've achieved or look like on the outside.

# But What If We're Wrong?

What would happen if you set out on this path and seven and a half years down the line of your fifteen-year journey you decided the frugal and investing life simply wasn't for you? Well, for starters, you wouldn't be the only one to call it quits. We've met plenty of people who've started their journey and completely given up along the way. They ascend to a height just below the cloudbreak and decide that the view from there is beautiful enough for them; there's no need to go further. To that we say cool.

You'll still have a little more than half a decade building valuable skills and discipline that will serve you for a lifetime. You'll likely also be part of the treasured minority of Americans who are debt-free, a feat worthy of celebration on its own. Shortly thereafter, you will have joined another minority group of Americans who can boast having a positive net worth. Assuming you'd consistently invested $10,000 into a tax-deferred account on an annual basis that grew at 7 percent, you'd have a portfolio balance in the ballpark of $90,000. Assuming you have no other assets and you're between the ages of eighteen and thirty-four, a $90,000 net worth places you higher than 80 percent of American families in your age-group.[1] If you're between the ages of thirty-five and forty-four, it places you higher than 55 percent of families in your age-group. And according to CNBC, a net worth of just $93,170 makes you richer than 90 percent of people worldwide.[2] Not bad—for a quitter.

But who do you become if you don't start at all?

Well, the answer to that question is pretty simple: almost everyone you've ever met. For the foreseeable future, you'll always be searching for a good or better job. You'll internalize sayings like "you have to work twice as hard for half as much" and perpetuate misinterpretations like "money is the root of all evil." You'll follow widely accepted advice like go to school, get a good job, and buy a house because that's what you're supposed to do. That's what's expected of you.

As you get older, you'll begin to sense that perhaps there were some things you could've done differently, but you'll suck it up because things could've been worse. And if you decide to have children, well, you'll give them the advice you were given because, in theory, it worked for you. You'll be sure to instill a strong work ethic in them and make sure they know in no uncertain terms that they didn't come from a rich family. And when they get old enough to earn income, you'll pass on a final financial lesson, one you hope they heed: save

10–15 percent, because "money doesn't grow on trees." At work, eventually you'll have a boss who's younger than you, and it'll feel as if they're an arrogant know-it-all. You'll grow increasingly frustrated as they try to change the way things have always been done. If you're lucky and likable, you'll adapt and hold on for a while longer. If not, you'll receive a legal- and human-resources-approved goodbye and maybe a slice of sheet cake.

If you haven't prepared for your financial future, life will be hard. If you've only moderately prepared, life will be comfortable, then hard. Either way, you'll eventually become the source of pressure your own children feel as they wrestle with their own set of financial decisions of whether to live for today or prepare to support you tomorrow. You'll hope for the government to pass legislation, and you'll wait to hear back from any given number of assistance programs. And the cycle will repeat itself.

That is the harsh reality of a growing number of people today, but it doesn't have to be. If you've gotten this far in the book, then we have some news for you: you've already started your transformation. We're confident that somewhere along the process of flipping through these pages or listening to this recording, you've already begun to question whether the commonly accepted career and financial path is an effective one. The stories shared in this book and the supporting evidence we've provided are pretty undeniable.

You should also know by now that knowing better does not always lead to doing better. Doing better requires bold action. Cashing out requires you to revisit your existing financial beliefs and give yourself a complete mental and emotional rewiring. To do this, you'll need to identify and discard the old rules of thumb and replace them with the new, flexible, modern, and effective rules and richuals we've provided you. You'll need to be clear about your financial picture and give a bold purpose to your current and future income. You'll need to accept that your career will end some day and that it's best for you to determine the end date, not your future boss. And as much as you give yourself credit for being a hard worker, you'll need to acknowledge that you could never work harder than your invested dollar can for you.

## The New Normal

For millions of Americans, 2020 will go down as a truly unforgettable year. When *The Washington Post* asked its readers to describe it using just one word, after thousands of responses the top results were "exhausting," "lost," "chaotic," "surreal," and "relentless."[3] Our social circles weren't nearly as eloquent, preferring terms like "dumpster fire," "shit show," and "hot mess" to describe what it felt like living through those twelve months. And for those who prefer visual definitions, memes and GIFs of people guzzling oversize cocktails while crying uncontrollably or simply staring into the abyss of their screens with bloodshot eyes summed up the year spent mostly inside.

Our feelings were no different, having spent the majority of the year in a daily battle against the intense sadness forced upon us by a global pandemic. Simple everyday acts like going to the grocery store, taking a walk, or opening mail became matters of life or death. As parents of a toddler, we struggled with the decision of whether to send our son to day care and assume the increased risk of COVID-19 exposure. Having been in day care for only a short while and having just begun to build his first relationships outside home, our son, like most kids, hated having to learn and socialize through a screen. He'd had a taste of what the world looked like outside the walls of our home, and he craved more of it.

As relatively new entrepreneurs, we were concerned about prospects as events, projects, and entire businesses were brought to their knees seemingly overnight. We'd planned to speak at large conferences, collaborate with major brands, and continue to build our business, but as the weeks turned to months, the opportunities faded away. As a married couple, we struggled to figure out how to support each other and our extended families when—not if—disaster struck close to home. We watched as private and public sector leaders scrambled to figure out what to do and say to provide a sense of calm during a truly unprecedented time. And as if that weren't enough, we lost beloved icons while emotionally fueled social protests spread during a contentious presidential election race. It felt as if the entire world were on fire, which made sense because, according to NASA, 2020 did in fact tie for the warmest year on record.[4]

*What did we learn during this time?* The answer is, we

learned and relearned the lessons outlined in this book. As business owners and investors, we saw that the importance of thinking "digital first" was paramount as we watched old institutions struggle with embracing new ways of serving customers and eventually going bankrupt. At the same time, we watched big tech grow and new tech players enter the mainstream as the world was forced to do everything online.

The year 2020 was the year many were forced to realize the future they'd heard of was at their doorstep, floating above them in a drone or maybe even in the cloud. Investors learned how incredibly unpredictable the stock market could be as we watched billions of dollars gained and lost like a seesaw. One tweet from a charismatic CEO, an unscrupulous act caught on a hot mic, or a viral social media moment could be the difference between someone earning or losing thousands in their portfolio.

The year 2020 was also the year that forced investors to finally decouple the health of the economy and the stock market. Gross domestic product, the single most widely used measure of economic health, fell by 3.5 percent compared with 2019—the worst decline since 1946.[5] Simultaneously, the S&P 500 index reached an all-time high, finishing the volatile year up over 16 percent.[6] In short, if you owned an index fund on January 1, 2020, the value of that holding would've grown more than twice the average historical rate by December 31, 2020, despite a dramatic decrease in our country's economic health.

As a married couple, we learned the art of forgiveness, because we both had front-row seats to each other's transformation in the face of chaos, volatility, and despair. We jostled back and forth as we were raising our son, trying to stay fit, and witnessing family and friends become infected with the virus, suffer layoffs, struggle with mental health, alcohol abuse, and domestic violence. During all this, we were trying to get some work done. The regularly scheduled webinars with our loved ones soon fell off the calendar in favor of texting as we all seemed to throw in the towel and sulk in solidarity. We found peace in the trusty 51 percent rule, believing that so long as we were happy just over half the time, we were winning. And we retreated to the claimed corners of our home with the exception of a daily meal, co-parenting, and, well, writing this book.

We were also reminded of how important it is to have a community of like-minded people in your corner. While there is no official record or unit of measurement of how those who've chosen to pursue the financial independence lifestyle fared, from our vantage point they, like us, were fine, because 2020 validated our preexisting beliefs and decisions. Long before the world shut down, this community had already done the deep work to detach their identities from their job titles. So, if a sudden layoff was forced upon them, it didn't throw them into a tailspin. In fact, it would've likely been welcomed, particularly if it came with a healthy severance package. They'd have already given their income a purpose, so they knew exactly what could be done with the sudden windfall of cash and time.

They were hardly affected by the sudden loss of a paycheck because they'd already established multiple streams or learned to live off far less than they made. The shutting down of the world around them didn't send them into chaos, because they'd already learned how to be self-sufficient and to enjoy the simpler things within the boundaries of their current standard of living. By and large, the money-smart community made the most of this watershed moment. Like anyone else, they tried new recipes, explored forgotten hobbies, binge-watched their favorite series, and maybe even read a few books. It may not sound like much of a difference from what you might have done except for one thing: they did it without worrying about money. The world had completely gone to shit around them, and for the vast majority of the financial independence community, it had little to no negative financial effect on their lives.

There were even a few in our community who went big and struck gold. In a single year, it was common to see people doubling their net worth in a few months. Having already achieved their target retirement numbers, some admittedly broke from the pack and bet big on individual stocks or tech-heavy index funds. And as you might imagine, they were rewarded handsomely by the market boom. As of the time of writing this book, the data isn't available quite yet, but we can safely assume many millionaires were born by betting big on companies like Tesla, Amazon, Apple, and Zoom in 2020. You'll likely read about them for years to come on popular financial media platforms, and some may even be celebrated as savvy multimillionaire investors and visionaries over the coming decade. We believe their accomplishments are noteworthy, and we particularly love to see how charitable they are with their winnings.

But those people—the upper crust—are only a tiny part of the financially independent community. The vast majority are rich and regular people like us. And perhaps most important for the everyday financially independent man and woman, 2020 revealed a handful of simpler, philosophical insights.

First, becoming a millionaire isn't an identity; it's hardly a worthwhile goal. It's merely an inevitable milestone achieved by people who invest steadily and consistently over time. Just as we understand that our bodies will eventually get tired after continuous exercise or that a ball thrown in the air will be brought down by gravity, we understand the inevitability of eclipsing the million-dollar milestone when money is invested and allowed to grow. And just as quickly, the market can decide to strip that milestone marker away from you without your having done anything different or wrong. Once you understand that, you understand that the title "millionaire" and the accompanying status that comes with it are worthless.

But if you must stake your claim on something, it should be on this second insight: appreciating the journey to achieving your stated financial goal. So many of the benefits people are really looking for can be utilized and experienced long before achieving their ultimate goal. Simply rising above financial insecurity can lift an enormous weight off your and your family's shoulders. Gaining financial flexibility can enable you to escape an unhealthy environment or even potentially dangerous life situation. Furthermore, you don't need to have achieved full financial independence or freedom to live a deeply meaningful, charitable, and fulfilling life. For most people, just being halfway there is enough to break the cycle of poverty in your family and be a role model within your chosen community.

And last, achieving financial independence is not a race or a competition. You don't win a gold star or trophy for doing it in record time. You're not better at it if you've paid off a greater amount of debt in a shorter period of time than others have. Your path is just that—yours.

When we first started on this path, the FIRE movement was in the early stages. As of the time of writing this book, it is still widely unknown, but the lifestyle has penetrated the mainstream media in spurts. The stories you've likely come across online and on television are extreme and mostly about people who've achieved remarkable wealth and gone to great lengths to get there. Do not be distracted by the ridiculous lengths many of those people have gone to to cut costs. Do not compare your abilities to save or invest with what those people have done either. We've found that the truest representation of this movement's impact is in the invisible stories—those deemed unworthy of major media coverage.

They're the stories of the couples who avoided divorce because they could afford to take vacations and truly unplug together. The story of the rock-star employee who hopped off the corporate ladder to prioritize their mental health, children, or caring for an aging parent. Or the stories of nonprofit organizations that achieved their funding goals by a handful of anonymous donors. All of these instances combined advance our families, influence policies, and improve our local communities.

That is what cashing out is all about.

# Acknowledgments

A wise woman once told us that writing a book is like having a child and that raising a child takes a village. So we'd like to take a moment to thank our village, who've lifted us up throughout this process.

To our loving parents, Blue, Cheryl, Sybil, and Vic, we can't thank you enough for your unwavering support through this process and throughout our lives. Thank you for serving as positive role models to us and others who aren't as fortunate to have parents like you. To our extended family and friends, your support of our relationship, business, and ideas is immeasurable. Thank you for pouring your hearts out to us over the years and for sharing your stories, history, joys, and heartbreak with us. Each and every one of you have informed and contributed to this body of work, whether you know it or not.

To the badass team of phenomenal women who helped this book come alive, Lucinda, Leah, Nina, and Niki; thank you so much for believing in us, sharing your expertise, and helping us to become published authors. You've made our wildest dreams come true, and you've helped us spread a message to a community of eager readers who need this push.

To the increasingly diverse voices, platforms, and families that consider themselves a part of the global FIRE movement, thank you for your open expressions of courage, transparency, generosity, and analysis. In our eyes, you are all pioneers and early adopters of an improved way of life—one that empowers workers, shatters rigged systems, and puts family first. Keep living by example, sharing your lessons with the world, and shaping the future one day at time.

And to the many working professionals who've shared their stories and aspirations for a better life with us—whether in person, via email, or on social media—we see you and we're rooting for you. If not for your exchanges, we wouldn't have been inspired to use our voices and skill sets to help others.

# APPENDIX

# Some Tips on Saving

I n the end, increasing your income will have a more tangible effect on your wealth than simply *decreasing* your spending. However, if you do need some help reining in your spending, we've curated some of our most useful tips on how to do this.

## Rules

*You don't have to save a flat percentage of your income every single month.* Given that your income and expenses may fluctuate throughout the year, it's okay to focus on an annual or quarterly target.

*If you are in purpose 2 (flexibility), aim to save 25 percent of your income if you're single and 50 percent if you live in a dual-income household.* Note, you don't have to do this forever, but a period of focused reduced spending over five to ten years can have a dramatic effect on your future.

*Find and contribute to a community that embraces sharing resources.* This includes everything from buying groceries/supplies in bulk, to carpooling, to tools, to children's clothing, to subscription services, to telephone plans, and so on.

# Richuals

*Broken down by budget category.*

## UTILITIES

*Be mindful of wasting energy, and if possible use tools and enhancements to regulate your usage.* This includes water filters on faucets, motion detectors on lights, smart thermostats, and energy-efficient appliances.

*Always choose variable plans so that you aren't paying for energy and resources you didn't use.* While it may be easier to predict how much your bill will be, a fixed-cost plan is almost always more expensive than the alternative.

*Be wary of saving tips provided by your service providers.* Oftentimes, they are indirectly trying to persuade you to use more, not less.

## HEALTH CARE

*Pay close attention during open-enrollment periods; don't just pick the cheapest policy.* Ensure that you look at the Plan Summary document to see the exact costs charged by the plan.

*Ask yourself the following questions beyond the plan's monthly premium:*

- Are your current doctors in network?
- Is the plan's network large enough that referrals can be covered in your area?
- Does the plan provide coverage while traveling or out of state?
- Does the plan cover prescription drugs, especially your current medications?
- How much are office visit co-pays? (Consider both primary care and specialists.)
- How much is the deductible?
- How much is the out-of-pocket maximum? Can you afford to pay it and your current expenses?
- Is there an opportunity to open a health savings account?
- Is there an employer contribution for a flexible spending account?

## TRANSPORTATION

*Aim to buy used cars that are functional, reliable, and fuel efficient.* Pay cash if you can, but if you have to finance a car, pay attention to the interest rate you are being charged on the loan, not the monthly car payment.

*Avoid buying premium gas unless your vehicle absolutely requires it according to manufacturer standards.*

*If possible, aim to have one vehicle per household.*

## FOOD

*Cooking at home is almost always a less expensive option compared with dining out or ordering in.*

*Learn to prepare and master dishes that reheat easily and are portable and versatile like stews, soups, rice dishes, and pasta.*

## CABLE

*Avoid expensive cable package bundles.* Instead, opt for à la carte streaming services using internet-connected devices. A full list of product recommendations can be found on our website, richandregular.com/resources.

*Watch your internet bill.* Unless you stream multiple high-definition videos, play video games online, or regularly use videoconferencing, you likely don't need the highest-speed internet. Whenever possible, choose the lowest speed/connection plan that still allows you to reasonably accomplish your tasks, and seek to own (not lease) the in-home equipment.

## INSURANCE

*Seek to bundle all of your insurance policies with a single, low-cost insurance provider.* Take advantage of the discount-rate opportunities for automatic payments, and if you can afford it, increase the deductibles to lower the overall cost of the premium.

*Revisit all policies on an annual basis to see if there are new features or discounts you are eligible for.*

*Do not assume that an insurance provider without mass media visibility (for example, advertising or brand sponsorships) is not a legitimate provider.* The larger providers with big marketing budgets are often more expensive than other available options.

*Choose term-life insurance over whole-life policies.*

## TELEPHONE

*Explore low-cost telephone service providers outside the most popular brands shown in the media.* Particularly if you work from home and can use internet service for telephone calls.

*Revisit all data and call plans on an annual basis to take advantage of available discounts and better packages.* Analyze your usage so you aren't buying into a plan that is larger and more expensive than you need.

## OTHER

*Personal care.* Take advantage of all free available options to maintain a healthy lifestyle that don't include membership. This includes walking, calisthenics, yoga, and cycling.

# Notes

## Chapter 1 | Your Wake-Up Call

1. Dedrick Asante-Muhammad et al., "The Road to Zero Wealth" (Washington, D.C.: Institute for Policy Studies, 2017).

## Chapter 2 | Rich and Regular

1. Hannah Sampson, "What Does America Have Against Vacation?," *Washington Post*, Aug. 28, 2019, www .washingtonpost.com/travel/2019/08/28 /what-does-america-have-against-vacation.
2. Jeanne Sahadi, "2019 Was a Record Year for CEO Turnover," CNN, Jan. 9, 2020, www.cnn.com/2020/01/09 /success/ceo-departures-record-high/index.html.
3. Pooja Jain-Link and Julia Taylor Kennedy, "Being Black in Corporate America," Coqual, Dec. 9, 2019, coqual.org /wp-content/uploads/2020/09 /CoqualBeingBlackinCorporateAmerica090720-1.pdf.
4. Asher Fergusson and Lyric Fergusson, "The 35 Best Countries to Raise a Family in 2020," Asher & Lyric, July 24, 2020, www.asherfergusson.com/raising-a-family-index.
5. OECD, Net Childcare Costs (indicator), accessed Jan. 31, 2021, doi:10.1787/e328a9ee-en.

6. Sean Braswell, "President Eisenhower's $14 Billion Heart Attack," OZY, April 12, 2016, www.ozy.com/true-and -stories/president-eisenhowers-14-billion-heart-attack /65157.

7. Chris Weller, "Japan Is Facing a 'Death by Overwork' Problem—Here's What It's All About," *Business Insider*, Oct. 18, 2017, www.businessinsider.com /what-is-karoshi-japanese-word-for-death-by-overwork -2017-10.

8. Faith Among Black Americans, Pew Research Center, Feb. 16, 2021, www.pewforum.org/2021/02/16/faith -among-black-americans.

### Chapter 3 | The Purpose(s) of Income

1. "It's in the Bag: Black Consumers' Path to Purchase," Nielsen Holdings, Sept. 12, 2019, www.nielsen.com/wp -content/uploads/sites/3/2019/09/2019-african-american -DIS-report.pdf.

2. Dedrick Asante-Muhammad et al., "The Road to Zero Wealth" (Washington, D.C.: Institute for Policy Studies, 2017).

3. "Consumer Expenditures—2019," U.S. Bureau of Labor Statistics, Sept. 9, 2020, www.bls.gov/news.release/cesan .nr0.htm.

4. Jessica Semega et al., "Income and Poverty in the United States: 2019" (Washington, D.C.: U.S. Government Publishing Office, 2020).

5. Colton Gardner, "Four Predictions About the Self-Storage Industry," *Forbes,* Nov. 25, 2019, www.forbes.com/sites /theyec/2019/11/25/four-predictions-about-the-self-storage -industry/?sh=32cd3fc47814.

6. "Median Size of U.S. Single Family House, 2000–2019," Statista, Nov. 24, 2020, www.statista.com/statistics/456925 /median-size-of-single-family-home-usa.

7. Wright, Ronald, *A Short History of Progress*. Toronto: Anasi, 2004

## Chapter 4 | *The Fifteen-Year Career*

1. German Lopez, "The Typical American Life, in One Chart," *Vox*, July 30, 2014, https://www.vox.com /2014/7/30/5951657/US-life-expectancy-marriage -birth-death.
2. U.S. Department of Education, National Center for Education Statistics, *Status and Trends in the Education of Racial and Ethnic Groups 2018* (NCES 2019-038), 2019, Degrees Awarded.
3. Liz Knueven, "The Average Student Loan Debt by Household Income, School Type, and Race," *Business Insider*, Aug. 21, 2020, www.businessinsider.com/personal -finance/average-student-loan-debt#how-to-pay-off-student -loan-debt.
4. National Law Center on Homelessness & Poverty, "Homelessness in American: Overview of Data and Causes," Jan. 2015.
5. "Nearly 40 Percent of Americans with Annual Incomes over $100,000 Live Paycheck-to-Paycheck," PR Newswire, Jan. 15, 2021, https://www.prnewswire.com/news-releases /nearly-40-percent-of-americans-with-annual-incomes-over -100-000-live-paycheck-to-paycheck-301312281.html.
6. The 1 percent rule suggests that gross rent collected should be at least 1 percent of the total price paid to secure the property. In other words, if we bought a home for $100,000, we should have been able to rent it for at least $1,000 a month.

## Chapter 6 | *Whatever You're Thinking, Think Bigger*

1. "Andrew Yang for Mayor of NYC—Forward New York," Yang for New York, accessed Feb. 4, 2021, www.yangforny .com.
2. David Baboolall et al., "Automation and the Future of the African American Workforce," McKinsey & Company, April 22, 2019, www.mckinsey.com/featured-insights /future-of-work/automation-and-the-future-of-the-african -american-workforce.

3. Andrew Perrin, "One-in-Five Americans Now Listen to Audiobooks," Pew Research Center, May 30, 2020, www .pewresearch.org/fact-tank/2019/09/25 /one-in-five-americans-now-listen-to-audiobooks.

4. Apjit Walia, "America's Racial Gap & Big Tech's Closing Window," Deutsche Bank Research, Sept. 3, 2020, www.dbresearch.com/PROD/RPS_EN-PROD /America%27s_Racial_Gap_%26_Big_Tech%27s_Closing _Window/RPS_EN_DOC_VIEW.calias?rwnode =PROD0000000000464258&ProdCollection =PROD0000000000511664.

5. Sarah Berger, "How This 35-Year-Old Dad Made $1.5 Million off a Simple Fiverr Side Hustle," CNBC, June 13, 2019, www.cnbc.com/2018/04/24/how-this-dad-made -almost-1-million-on-fiverr.html.

6. Jenny Singer, "Stacey Abrams Is the Author of Eight Unapologetically Hot Romance Novels," *Glamour*, Dec. 3, 2020, www.glamour.com/story/stacey-abrams-is-a-published -romance-novelist-and-her-books-are-fabulous.

7. Reid Cramer, "The Emerging Millennial Wealth Gap," New America, accessed Feb. 5, 2021, www.newamerica.org /millennials/reports/emerging-millennial-wealth-gap /framing-the-millennial-wealth-gap-demographic -realities-and-divergent-trajectories.

8. Peter Gosselin, "If You're over 50, Chances Are the Decision to Leave a Job Won't Be Yours," ProPublica, Dec. 28, 2018, www.propublica.org/article/older-workers-united-states -pushed-out-of-work-forced-retirement.

9. "2020 Racial Wage Gap—Compensation Research from PayScale," PayScale, accessed Feb. 5, 2021, www.payscale .com/data/racial-wage-gap.

## Chapter 7 | *Put Your Money to Work*

1. Matthew Frankel, "What's the Average American's Tax Rate?," The Motley Fool, March 4, 2017, www.fool.com /retirement/2017/03/04/whats-the-average-americans-tax -rate.aspx.

2. "SPIVA Scorecard," New York, June 2020, www.spindices .com/spiva/#/reports.

3. Sunita Sah, George Loewenstein, and Daylian Cain, "Insinuation Anxiety: Concern That Advice Rejection Will Signal Distrust After Conflict of Interest Disclosures," *Personality and Social Psychology Bulletin* 45, no. 7 (2019): 1099–1112, www.cmu.edu/dietrich/sds/docs/loewenstein /insinuation-anxiety.pdf.

4. Drew Desilver, "For Most U.S. Workers, Real Wages Have Barely Budged in Decades," Pew Research Center, Aug. 7, 2018, www.pewresearch.org/fact-tank/2018/08/07/for -most-us-workers-real-wages-have-barely-budged-for -decades.

5. Louise Story, "Anywhere the Eye Can See, It's Likely to See an Ad," *New York Times*, Jan. 15, 2007, https://www.nytimes .com/2007/01/15/business/media/15everywhere.html.

## Chapter 8 | The He Said/She Said Dance

1. Kelsey Borresen, "The Psychological Benefits of Having Things to Look Forward To," *HuffPost*, May 21, 2020, www.huffpost.com/entry/psychological-benefits-things-look -forward-to_l_5ec40575c5b62696fb60e3a1.

2. "Marriage and Divorce," American Psychological Association, accessed Feb. 3, 2021, www.apa.org/topics /divorce-child-custody.

## Chapter 9 | Find Your FI Community

1. Richard G. Gardner et al., "'I Must Have Slipped Through the Cracks Somehow': An Examination of Coping with Perceived Impostorism and the Role of Social Support," *Journal of Vocational Behavior* 115 (Dec. 2019), www .sciencedirect.com/science/article/pii/S0001879119301095.

2. "Community of Practice," Wikiwand, accessed Feb. 5, 2021, www.wikiwand.com/en/Community_of_practice.

3. Etienne Wenger-Trayner and Beverly Wenger-Trayner, "Introduction to Communities of Practice," Wenger, 2015, wenger-trayner.com/introduction-to-communities-of-practice.

### Conclusion: But What If We're Wrong?

1. Quoctrung Bui, Kevin Quealy, and Rumsey Taylor, "Are You Rich? Where Does Your Net Worth Rank in America?," *New York Times,* Aug. 12, 2019, www.nytimes.com /interactive/2019/08/12/upshot/are-you-rich-where-does -your-net-worth-rank-wealth.html.

2. Kathleen Elkins, "Here's How Much Money It Takes to Be Among the Richest 50 Percent of People Worldwide," CNBC, Nov. 19, 2018, www.cnbc.com/2018/11/19/how-much -money-it-takes-to-be-among-the-richest-50-percent -worldwide.html.

3. Eliza Goren, Shefali S. Kulkarni, and Kanyakrit Vongkiatkajorn, "'Exhausting,' 'Surreal,' 'Dumpster Fire': How Our Readers Described 2020," *Washington Post,* Dec. 18, 2020, www.washingtonpost.com/graphics/2020 /lifestyle/2020-in-one-word.

4. Katherine Brown, "2020 Tied for Warmest Year on Record, NASA Analysis Shows," NASA, Jan. 14, 2021, www.nasa .gov/press-release/2020-tied-for-warmest-year-on-record -nasa-analysis-shows.

5. Anneken Tappe, "Donald Trump's Final Economic Report Card Could Be Very Underwhelming," CNN, Jan. 27, 2021, www.cnn.com/2021/01/27/economy/us-gdp-fourth-quarter -preview/index.html.

6. Apjit Walia, "America's Racial Gap & Big Tech's Closing Window," Deutsche Bank Research, Sept. 3, 2020, www .dbresearch.com/PROD/RPS_EN-PROD/America%27s _Racial_Gap_%26_Big_Tech%27s_Closing_Window/RPS _EN_DOC_VIEW.calias?rwnode=PROD0000 000000464258&ProdCollection=PROD000000 0000511664.

# Index

Note: Italicized page numbers indicate material in tables or illustrations.